Carrella

PRAISE FOR THE PLAYS OF ADAM RAPP

ESSENTIAL SELF-DEFENSE

"Rapp is a latter-day incarnation of Sam Shepard . . . [*Essential Self-Defense* is] an entertaining tall tale of fear and loathing in Midwestern America." —JOHN LAHR, *The New Yorker*

"This fresh and muscular voice [has] no fear . . . The journey is full of oddball joy." —LINDA WINER, *Newsday*

RED LIGHT WINTER

"Complex and compelling . . . What at first glance appeared to be a study of friendship turns, by degrees, into an exploration of passion and the perverse . . . [Rapp] has a generous talent. In *Red Light Winter*, he brings memorable news about the heart, telling us both how it fools itself and how it kills itself." —JOHN LAHR, *The New Yorker*

"An arresting study in melancholic triangulation and obsessions dashed . . . Shrewd about the way certain male friendships exist on the knife edge of disaster." —MICHAEL PHILLIPS, *Chicago Tribune*

"A tight two-act portrait of toxic male rivalry, sexual obsession and treacherous memory . . . This intense character study will amuse, arouse, shock and devastate you . . . A wildly engrossing tale of violent desire, from a passionate writer making good on his early promise." —DAVID COTE, *Time Out New York*

"A frank, graphic story of erotic fixation and the havoc it can wreak on sensitive souls, [this play] marks a step forward for Mr. Rapp . . . [,] here exploring a wider range of human emotion and writing with a new sensitivity to match his natural gift for crackling, hyperarticulate dialogue."

—CHARLES ISHERWOOD, *The New York Times*

STONE COLD DEAD SERIOUS

"Rapp is very gifted, and, even rarer, he has something to say . . . *Stone Cold Dead Serious* [is] brave, compassionate, and at times . . . breathtakingly moving."

—BRUCE WEBER, *The New York Times*

"Sharp and disquieting . . . Beneath the scurrilous comic banter and absurd surfaces is a mysterious recurrence of objects, actions, persona and language, in an oblique and haunting style reminiscent of Haruki Murakami's best fiction."

—ED PARK, *The Village Voice*

"[A] scabrous, poignant vision of suburban-American innocence lost." —CAROLYN CLAY, *The Boston Phoenix*

"Will leave your mind buzzing and your heart aching."

—BRANDON WOLCOTT, *Show Business*

FASTER

"Talented and highly prolific . . . Rapp . . . is brave and facile in his language, and he ventures where few writers are able or willing to go."   —BRUCE WEBER, *The New York Times*

"There's no want of energy [in] *Faster* . . . [Rapp] has a rising reputation for creating fast-talking, hard-hitting characters who make up in colorful language and intensity what they lack in, well, social graces."   —JEREMY GERARD, *New York*

"[Rapp] has made a name for himself writing about the darker things . . . *Faster* is no exception as it examines the complex relationship between hope and reality, faith and circumstance."

—RANEE JABER, *Show Business*

FINER NOBLE GASES

"Rapp boldly and honestly exposes a segment of society that most of us, thankfully, know only from a distance. [*Finer Noble Gases*] is a resounding warning about what happens when parents disconnect from their children and the young turn to drugs, television and other substances as emotional pacifiers."

—JUDITH EGERTON, *The Courier-Journal* (Louisville)

"These aren't your typical alienated hipsters. Mr. Rapp is aiming for something much more grand and metaphysical than just another mundane tale of arrested development."

—JASON ZINOMAN, *The New York Times*

"Rockers Chase . . . and Staples . . . are a present-day Vladimir and Estragon—hoboes with nowhere to go, waiting indefinitely for someone to rescue them . . . Given Rapp's view of slackerdom as a kind of installation art, [the play] helps turn what feels like nothing into something of hypnotic beauty."

—DAVID NG, *The Village Voice*

NOCTURNE

"A startling, unnerving work of art that fiercely pushes the boundaries of theater . . . Rapp is an original—a distinctive voice . . . *Nocturne* will haunt you for a long time."

—MICHAEL KUCHWARA, Associated Press

"A brilliant, terrifying, perceptive, occasionally funny play . . . Bold, daring and successful." —DONALD LYONS, *New York Post*

"Adam Rapp's *Nocturne* is remarkable enough to bear comparisons with Margaret Edson's award-winning *Wit* . . . Here [is] a playwright . . . to watch with keen interest."

—MARKLAND TAYLOR, *Variety*

ADAM RAPP
THE METAL CHILDREN

ADAM RAPP has been the recipient of a Herbert H. and Patricia M. Brodkin Scholarship; two Lecomte du Noüy awards; a fellowship to the Camargo Foundation in Cassis, France; a Roger L. Stevens Award from the Kennedy Center Fund for New American Plays; a Suite Residency with Mabou Mines; the Helen Merrill Award for Emerging Playwrights; Boston's Elliot Norton Award; a 2006 Princess Grace Statue Award; a Lucille Lortel Playwright's Fellowship; and the 2007 Benjamin H. Danks Award from the American Academy of Arts and Letters. He was short-listed for the William Saroyan International Prize for Writing for *Nocturne*, and he received a Joseph Jefferson Award in Chicago for Best New Play, received a special citation from the Obies, and was a finalist for the Pulitzer Prize for Drama for *Red Light Winter*.

His plays include *Ghosts in the Cottonwoods* (Victory Gardens; Arcola Theatre, London); *Animals and Plants* (American Repertory Theater); *Blackbird* (Bush Theatre, London; City Theatre, Pittsburgh; Off-Broadway at Edge Theater); *Nocturne* (American

Repertory Theater, Off-Broadway at New York Theatre Workshop); *Stone Cold Dead Serious* (American Repertory Theater, Off-Broadway at Edge Theater); *Finer Noble Gases* (26th Annual Humana Festival of New American Plays, Off-Broadway at Rattlestick Playwrights Theater); *Faster* (Off-Broadway at Rattlestick); *Trueblinka* (Off-Broadway at the Maverick Theater); *Dreams of the Salthorse* (Encore Theatre Company, San Francisco); *Red Light Winter* (Steppenwolf; Off-Broadway at the Barrow Street Theater); *Gompers* (City Theatre, Pittsburgh; Arcola Theatre, London); *American Sligo* (Off-Broadway at Rattlestick Playwrights Theater); *Bingo with the Indians* (Off-Broadway at the Flea Theater); and *Kindness* (Playwrights Horizons).

Trade editions of his plays, all available from Faber and Faber, include *Nocturne, Stone Cold Dead Serious and Other Plays, Red Light Winter,* and *Essential Self-Defense.*

He is the writer and director of two feature films: *Winter Passing,* starring Ed Harris, Will Ferrell, and Zooey Deschanel, which premiered at the 2005 Toronto International Film Festival; and *Blackbird.*

He is the author of seven novels for young adults: *Missing the Piano; The Buffalo Tree; The Copper Elephant; Little Chicago; 33 Snowfish; Under the Wolf, Under the Dog,* which was a finalist for the Los Angeles Times Book Prize; and *Punkzilla.* He is also the author of the adult novel *The Year of Endless Sorrows* (Farrar, Straus and Giroux) and the graphic novel *Ball Peen Hammer.*

A graduate of Clarke College in Dubuque, Iowa, Mr. Rapp also completed a two-year playwriting fellowship at Juilliard. He lives in New York City.

THE METAL CHILDREN

THE METAL CHILDREN

A play by **ADAM RAPP**

FABER AND FABER, INC.

An affiliate of Farrar, Straus and Giroux   New York

FABER AND FABER, INC.
An affiliate of Farrar, Straus and Giroux
18 West 18th Street, New York 10011

Copyright © 2010 by Adam Rapp
Distributed in Canada by D&M Publishers, Inc.
Printed in the United States of America
First edition, 2010

Library of Congress Cataloging-in-Publication Data
Rapp, Adam.
    The metal children : a play / by Adam Rapp. — 1st ed.
        p.   cm.
    ISBN 978-0-86547-924-1 (pbk. : alk. paper)
    1. Prohibited books—Drama.   2. City and town life—Drama.
3. Middle West—Drama.   I. Title.

PS3568.A6278M48 2009
812'.54—dc22

                                                           2009041808

Designed by Abby Kagan

www.fsgbooks.com

1   3   5   7   9   10   8   6   4   2

FOR K.

ACKNOWLEDGMENTS

The author would like to thank Sarah Stern, Jen Garvey-Blackwell, and Doug Aibel from the Vineyard Theatre for their belief in this play. Doug Aibel's notes throughout every phase of development have been invaluable. He would also like to thank all the actors who performed the workshop production in June 2008: Michael Shannon, David Greenspan, Halley Wegryn-Gross, Betsy Aidem, Mia Dillon, Connor Barrett, Katherine Waterston, Kerry Bishé, and Guy Boyd. David Greenspan beautifully performed a character that was ultimately cut from the play, and for his work the author is especially grateful. The author would also like to thank Todd Haimes of the Roundabout Theatre Company for commissioning the play. And last but not least, the author would like to thank his agent, the unflappable John Buzzetti, for not giving up on this one, even when it was a big fat mess.

INTRODUCTION

In the spring of 2005, I received a call from Bruce Weber of *The New York Times* telling me he was about to travel to Reading, Pennsylvania, where my young adult novel *The Buffalo Tree* had caused a bit of a stir. The novel, published by Front Street in 1997, was a part of the English curriculum at Muhlenberg High School, and a young woman, purportedly "puppeteered" by a local Christian group, quoted passages from the novel containing sexual content and foul language in front of the local school board. The book was immediately pulled off the shelves and wrested from student hands, and all copies were banished to a large vault.

Mr. Weber told me there was going to be a town meeting to discuss the improper procedure implemented in banning the book. He said that the major players on both sides would be present and asked me if I was going to attend. This was certainly a shock to me. I couldn't go. I was in Chicago and about to start tech rehearsals for the world premiere of my play *Red Light Winter* at Steppenwolf. We'd only had three and a half weeks of rehearsal and I was directing. This isn't much time to get a production up to speed, and I told Mr. Weber as much. He called me from the meeting and put one of the students on the phone with me. She had apparently stood up in front of her community and offered her copy, which she owned, to the library so that other kids could continue reading the book. She was extremely excited to talk to me, and I was moved to tears.

Incidentally, *Red Light Winter* opened without a glitch, and all was good in Chicago. Bruce Weber went on to publish an article about *The Buffalo Tree* and the controversy at Muhlenberg High School in *The New York Times*. The book remained off the reading list, which saddened me. I was grateful that he gave the matter so much attention. I cut the article out of the newspaper and put it all behind me.

A year later, that same community in Pennsylvania called for another meeting to discuss where things were at with regard to the book, how the decision to keep it off the reading list affected students and teachers, and how the whole experience was possibly changing the way reading materials were selected for English class. I was contacted by the courageous progressive teacher who was leading the charge in favor of *The Buffalo Tree*, and he invited me to be part of the conversation. I agreed to come, and when I arrived in Reading, I met with all the major players on both sides of the issue. There was a dinner at the house of the provost of the local college. It was all very civil. The food was good. I was nervous.

The actual meeting was held in a Lutheran church. There was a large banquet table set up on the altar, with pitchers of water and Styrofoam cups. Organ music was played while people filed in. I was placed at the center of the table. On either side of me were people who either loved or hated the book. The plan was to hear the various points of view of the people seated at the table, and then the public would have an opportunity to ask questions and share their opinions.

When I was asked to speak, I did so from a pulpit. No one else had to do that, but it was offered to me and I took it. I had nothing prepared. I heard myself saying things about never wanting to hurt anyone and not having any real intentions for the book beyond telling the story of a young boy who was trying to survive his brief but brutal stay in a reform school. I felt like I was speaking passionately, but I also felt far away from my own material. I'd written the book in 1995, after all—eleven years earlier. I remembered the characters' names and most of the significant action. I told the audience I really had been interested in writing about survival and mercy and loyalty; that it was a violent world I was dealing with, but no more violent than the stuff we see in the streets, on TV, on the Internet. I told them how hard it had been to write the book; that it was personal, drawn from some of my own experiences when I was sent to reform school for half of the fifth grade. But with many of the specifics in the novel, there was a kind of amnesia at play, and it was this memory loss that haunted me as I took the train back to New York.

I started to think about how a piece of art, specifically a work of literature, can have its own life. The book itself—the artifact—can gain a power completely independent of that of its creator. *The Buffalo Tree* received some nice reviews when it was published, and it went on to be named a 1997 School Library Journal Best Book for Young Adults, but it was by no means a bestseller. It has managed to stay in print, but my royalty checks—the few that I've seen for it—can barely pay my rent. I moved on from that novel and wrote more. And I've written plays and a few films and television scripts. I was stunned that the book was causing such a mess eleven years after the first printing. And I was sad that the book had drifted from my memory.

Many other things had happened that evening in Reading. One brave student approached a lectern that was placed in the center aisle of the church and confronted the head of the school board, asking him why he felt he could make decisions about what kids were capable of processing with regard to sex and violence when he'd never even spoken to one single student and had little or no presence in the high school. About a hundred students stood up and cheered, and the hair on the back of my neck stood up. A standing ovation at curtain call doesn't even come close to what I felt at that moment.

I decided I wanted to write a play about a book, which is a strange thing to do, because books aren't people and they don't *do* anything. As far as objects go, they are about as passive as it gets. As I started the play, I realized I was actually writing about people. I was writing about a lost writer and impassioned teenagers and a loving aunt and a precocious sixteen-year-old girl who grew up in a motel.

The book within the play (titled *The Metal Children*) is about a rash of teenage pregnancies and what that does to a small town in the heartland.

In some ways, the play *The Metal Children* is a fantasy of what I was expecting in Reading. It is part nightmare, part old-fashioned wish, and my attempt to meditate on both sides of an issue that means a lot to me: kids reading books. I've always believed that kids are much wiser than we think they are and that to deprive them of complex expressions of art because of violence or sexual content is to condescend to them.

In writing this play, I've also found that the works we move on from, whether novels, plays, or poems, come back to haunt us in ways that are hard to articulate. They are like wandering . . . well, children, who never grow up, who periodically come in out of the cold and make us look into their enormous, wondering eyes. They leave us alone for a while and we love them from a strange distance.

In preparation for the workshop production of *The Metal Children*, I reread *The Buffalo Tree*, and when I'd finished I honestly couldn't decide whether it was appropriate for all kids who are fourteen and up, as it says on the back of the book. I don't have kids. I think that in some ways I have never grown up, and therefore I consider myself good source material, but the closest I have come to parenting has been raising my three-year-old dog, Cesar, who happens not to read and, in fact, speaks very little English. But if I had a little girl or boy, perhaps I would find the content of *The Buffalo Tree* salacious and unnecessarily violent. Therefore it was important to me to discuss both sides of the issue, to not dismiss those who are against the novel within the play (*The Metal Children*), and as the play *The Metal Children* has developed, I have done my best to honor this intention.

ADAM RAPP

THE METAL CHILDREN

The Metal Children was originally presented as a Lab Production by the Vineyard Theatre (Douglas Aibel, artistic director; Jen Garvey-Blackwell, executive director). The first performance was on June 10, 2008. The sets were designed by Charlie Corcoran, the lights by Tyler Micelou, the costumes by Daphne Javich, the sound by Eric Shimelonis, and the props by Jay Duckworth. The production stage manager was Megan Smith, and the assistant director was Erika Christensen. It was directed by the author, and the cast was as follows:

TOBIN FALMOUTH	*Michael Shannon*
BRUNO BINELLI/PERRY WALDVOGEL	*David Greenspan*
KONG/TAMI LAKE/BOY X	*Halley Wegryn-Gross*
LYNNE/ROBERTA CUPP	*Betsy Aidem*
EDITH DUNDEE	*Mia Dillon*
STACEY KINSELLA	*Connor Barrett*
VERA DUNDEE	*Katherine Waterston*
COOPER/NURSE/BOY IN PORKY PIG MASK	*Kerry Bishé*
OTTO HURLEY	*Guy Boyd*

The world premiere of *The Metal Children* was produced at the Vineyard Theatre (Douglas Aibel, artistic director; Jen Garvey-Blackwell, executive director). The first performance was on May 17, 2010. The sets were designed by David Korins, the lights by Ben Stanton, and the sound by Eric Shimelonis. The costume designer, production stage manager, and assistant director were not yet determined as the book went to press. The play was directed by the author, and the cast was as follows:

TOBIN FALMOUTH	*Billy Crudup*
BRUNO BINELLI	*David Greenspan*
KONG/TAMI LAKE/BOY X	*Halley Wegryn-Gross*
LYNNE/ROBERTA CUPP	*Betsy Aidem*
EDITH DUNDEE	*Susan Blommaert*
STACEY KINSELLA	*Connor Barrett*
VERA DUNDEE	*Phoebe Strole*
COOPER/NURSE/BOY IN	
PORKY PIG MASK	*Jessy Hodges*
OTTO HURLEY	*Guy Boyd*

Note: The role of Perry Waldvogel, originally part of the Lab Production, was cut for the world premiere.

CHARACTERS

TOBIN FALMOUTH, a novelist in his late thirties, disheveled, adrift

BRUNO BINELLI, a feisty gay Italian-American book agent, mid-forties

KONG, a teenage male pot dealer; a skater punk homeboy

LYNNE, a woman of fifty who likes to party; tired

EDITH DUNDEE, a woman in her fifties who runs a roadside motel; sweet

STACEY KINSELLA, a progressive high school English teacher in his mid-thirties, at once fearless and terrified

VERA DUNDEE, a young woman of sixteen; a precocious visionary

COOPER, a young woman of sixteen; Vera's second-in-command

BOY IN PORKY PIG MASK, a teenage boy; a bully

OTTO HURLEY, a civic leader with a big booming voice, fifties

TAMI LAKE, a young Christian woman of sixteen, God-fearing

ROBERTA CUPP, a community leader of the Christian right, mid-forties; a widow

NURSE, a young woman with a firm bedside manner

BOY X, a high school freshman with an unusually high sperm count; eager to please

TIME

The present

PLACE

An apartment in New York City
Midlothia, a small town in the heartland

ACT I

SCENE 1

A one-bedroom apartment in the West Village that looks as if a bookmobile and a roving, high-speed Salvation Army float had collided on top of some tasteful Pottery Barn furniture. A small kitchen nook with a counter that divides it from the living space. There is a barely functioning fish tank, with one live fish and at least one dead one. There are also a few expired plants and scores of makeshift ashtrays scattered here and there. At one time, it was probably a pretty nice apartment.

TOBIN FALMOUTH, *late thirties, is seated on his congested sofa in the living room. A camcorder has been set up in front of him, and he is clutching a piece of paper. He wears boxer shorts, mismatched socks, a stained white T-shirt, and an old, light blue terry cloth bathrobe. His hair is a mess. He needs a shave. He regards the camcorder for a moment, clears his throat, and then begins to read from the piece of paper.*

TOBIN Um, Hi. My name is Tobin Falmouth. I am talking to you from my apartment in New York City. I apologize for the mess. With regard to my current state, lately things have been a little, well, "shoddy" would be the word, I suppose. Shoddy at best.

I am the author of *The Metal Children*, a young adult novel that was published by Frontage Road Press in 1997. It's my second published novel, the second of four. It has recently been brought to my attention that certain members of your community have taken issue with my book. I am aware of the events of a recent school board meeting at which a disgruntled student read some carefully selected quotes in front of your five-member committee.

The bathroom door is flung open, and BRUNO BINELLI, TOBIN*'s agent, storms out. He is in his mid-forties, a feisty gay Italian American. He wears a nice suit and tie, nice shoes, a good haircut.*

BRUNO I've felt more passion from a can opener. At least pretend like you have a point of view.

TOBIN Who are you all of a sudden—Uta Hagen?

BRUNO Tobin, do you have any idea what this might mean to these people? The least you could do is read it with a shred of enthusiasm.

TOBIN But I didn't even write it.

BRUNO What, my prose isn't fucking purple enough for you?

TOBIN Your prose is fine, Bruno. It's just—I don't know—I'm not an actor.

BRUNO You don't have to be a fucking *actor*; you just have to fucking *mean it*. And don't apologize for the messy apartment; you're a novelist.

BRUNO *exits to the bathroom.* TOBIN *resets the camera, begins.*

TOBIN (*with slightly more feeling*) Hi. My name is Tobin Falmouth. I am talking to you from my apartment in New York City. As you can see, I am a profound slob. But according to my well-groomed agent, who is currently sweltering in my three-by-five bathroom, this should be of no consequence because I am a novelist.

BRUNO (*from behind the bathroom door*) I'm editing that!

TOBIN (*barreling on*) In fact, I am the author of *The Metal Children*, a young adult novel that was published by Frontage Road Press in 1997. I can also make origami cranes, a rather potent mint julep, and a halfway decent western omelet, but I digress. Back to the script . . .

The Metal Children was my second published novel, the second of four in a mildly uneventful, slightly depressing career riddled with artistic impotence. Just kidding. (*back on the script*) It has recently been brought to my attention that certain members of your community have taken issue with *The Metal Children*. I am aware of the events of a recent school board meeting at which a disgruntled student read some carefully selected quotes in front of your five-member committee. I also learned that upon hearing the quoted material, albeit out of context, the committee decided that the book be immediately struck from the curriculum and that without following proper procedure, several paperback copies of *The Metal Children* were then confiscated from readers, taken out of classrooms, seized from library shelves, and placed in a sealed vault. (*to* BRUNO) Nice peppering of active verbs!

(*back to the script*) I am speaking to you now so that I may shed some light on what my intentions were in writing the novel. First I must say that I have never considered myself to be—

The buzzer sounds. TOBIN *stops the camcorder, crosses to his intercom, answers.*

TOBIN Hello?
VOICE (*VO*) It's Kong.

TOBIN *buzzes* KONG *in.* BRUNO *enters from the bathroom.*

BRUNO *Kong?*
TOBIN Relax. This'll just take a sec.

A knock on the door. TOBIN *crosses, opens the door.* KONG, *a somewhat androgynous white teen, dressed like a hip-hop skater punk, enters, carrying a book bag. He eases into the room a bit suspicious of* BRUNO.

TOBIN That's Bruno. He's my agent. (*to* BRUNO) Bruno, Kong.
BRUNO Hidy.
KONG (*to* TOBIN) Why you got a agent—you a actor?
TOBIN Writer.
KONG Word?
BRUNO Several hundred *thousand* words, actually.

From his book bag, KONG *removes several small, multicolored terrariums of high-quality hydroponic marijuana, sets them on the floor.*

KONG What kinda stuff you write?

BRUNO He writes very powerful and provocative novels.

KONG A novel's like a book, right?

BRUNO A published work of fiction, yes.

TOBIN *picks up each terrarium, turning it in the light, studying their crystals, etc.* BRUNO *watches the proceedings suspiciously.*

KONG (*referring to one of the terrariums*) That's the hoobily-doobily right there, yo. Smell it.

TOBIN *removes the top, smells it.*

KONG What about you, B.?

BRUNO What about me?

KONG You like the hoobily-doobily?

TOBIN I'll take this one.

KONG Word.

KONG *goes to work retrieving the other terrariums, putting them back in his book bag.* TOBIN *produces eighty dollars.* KONG *counts it quickly.*

KONG Thanks, yo. I'm out. (*to* BRUNO) Nice to meet you,
Pluto.

BRUNO Bruno.

KONG I mean Bruno.

KONG *exits.* BRUNO *is shaking his head.*

TOBIN What?

BRUNO The hoobily-doobily? No wonder you're nine months
late on the new book.

TOBIN Look, Bruno, I don't need you judging me right now.

BRUNO I'm not judging you, I'm just concerned.

LYNNE, *a middle-aged woman, enters. She is disoriented, hung
over, almost attractive, beat to shit, smoking a cigarette. She has
nicotine teeth and a tattoo or two. She wears a sheet and maybe
some tube socks. She and* BRUNO *share a look.*

TOBIN Hey, Lynne.

LYNNE Who's he?

BRUNO I'm General Robert E. Lee. I like hang gliding,
mountain biking, and playing the helicon tuba.

TOBIN His name is Bruno.

LYNNE Nice suit, Bruno. (*to* TOBIN) Hey, Toby, you seen my
keys?

He crosses to the fish tank, reaches inside, grabs her keys.

LYNNE (*referring to the camcorder*) What's this for?

TOBIN I'm making an official statement.

LYNNE Like a speech?

BRUNO Tobin wrote a novel that has recently caused quite a stir in a community in the American heartland.

LYNNE The heartland, huh? What kinda stir?

BRUNO A small but potent right-wing contingent is lobbying to strike it from the high school curriculum. Next week they're having a school board meeting to discuss the fate of the book, and he's making a video statement that they can play at the meeting.

LYNNE You're a writer? (*to* BRUNO) I thought he sold knives.

BRUNO You sell knives?

LYNNE He sold me a Yellowhorse Sacred Eagle Spirit Blade for three hundred bucks. (*to* TOBIN) I don't know how you suckered me into that—I musta been loaded.

BRUNO That knife was a gift, Tobin!

LYNNE Wait. Are you two like . . . ?

TOBIN Bruno's my agent.

BRUNO (*to* TOBIN, *genuinely hurt*) Who *are* you?

TOBIN *exits.* LYNNE *smokes for a moment.*

LYNNE (*to* TOBIN, *off*) So what's your book about, Toby?

BRUNO It's about a small town in the Midwest where a group of pregnant teenagers are mysteriously disappearing, one by one. And following each disappearance, a statue of the missing girl appears in a barren cornfield.

LYNNE Freaky. What's it called?

BRUNO It's called *The Metal Children*. It was named a 1997 Best Book for Young Adults and was short-listed for the L.A. Times Book Prize.

TOBIN *enters with a toothbrush in a glass of orange juice, brushes his teeth over the following.*

LYNNE Wow, Toby, I'm impressed. I really thought you sold knives. (*to* BRUNO) I mean, what a fuckin' trip, right? You think you know someone . . . (*to* TOBIN) See you around, Mr. Mystery Man.

She exits. BRUNO *watches him for a moment.*

TOBIN What? She lives downstairs.

BRUNO Did you have sex with her?

No answer.

BRUNO You did, didn't you? You fucking had sex with her!

TOBIN So?

BRUNO What's *wrong* with you?

TOBIN You know I'm lonely, Bruno.

BRUNO Did you use a condom?

TOBIN (*lying*) Of course.

BRUNO No, you didn't! Jesus! . . . Look, Tobin. There's a community out there that is up in arms about your book.

Hundreds of people are fighting for the life of your greatest achievement to date.

TOBIN Bruno, please. Hundreds of people?

BRUNO I have a photocopy of a petition with over three hundred student signatures on it. Three hundred and twelve to be exact. I have fourteen pages of a heated blog debate.

TOBIN Ooh, a heated blog—

BRUNO Shut up! . . . Now, I'm going to read you something, and I want you to listen, you smug, unappreciative prick!

BRUNO *produces a letter, unfolds it, reads.*

BRUNO It's dated March fourteenth, three days ago . . .

Dear Mr. Falmouth,
My name is Stacey Kinsella, and I'm the English Department chairperson at Midlothia Memorial High School, the site of a recent tragedy that altered the course of reading experiences for many. I'm also a teacher who strongly believes in the power of young adult literature.
At a time in their lives when most students are making crucial life decisions, Meredith Miller's redemptive journey in The Metal Children *provides positive moral guidance and future hope. It's simply the most amazingly written novel for young adults I've ever read.*
I apologize for not contacting you sooner, but I've been busy working on the book's defense. In truth, it has been an easy, if time-consuming, task. The voices of students past and

present, as well as my own reader's perceptions, led me to the many relevant themes contemporary youth can connect to their own lives: the failure of parents to educate youth, friendship, suicide, sympathy, fighting injustice, broken homes, coming of age, sexual awareness, body image, and the power of the human spirit to survive the most trying of circumstances. Clearly I do not want to lose this book. There are too many adolescent lives at stake.

On Wednesday, March twenty-fourth, I will be presenting my defense of The Metal Children *at an open school board meeting at the Midlothia Memorial High School auditorium, scheduled for seven-thirty in the evening. Equally passionate educators, students, and community members will be there, along with local media coverage. If there is any way that you can attend this meeting, I know it will do much to lift the spirits of all of us fighting for the book.*

Before I close, I want to thank you for writing such a beautiful novel. Its words remind me to seek out my own inner strength in this time of crisis. And like your young heroine, Meredith Miller, my fists are clenched and my heart is open.

> *Sincerely,*
> *Stacey Kinsella*
> *Midlothia Memorial High School*

TOBIN She sounds hot. Do you think she's hot?

BRUNO Tobin, my advice to you is get on a plane. Take a few days out of your precious life and go to that school board meeting. Reconnect with your audience. Look them in the eye. You haven't even left this apartment in over a month. I promise you it'll do you a world of good.

TOBIN Bruno, I'm broke.

BRUNO I'll buy you your ticket.

TOBIN I don't like flying.

BRUNO I'll fucking rent you a car.

TOBIN Really?

BRUNO Yes.

TOBIN Like an SUV?

BRUNO Whatever you want, Tobin.

TOBIN Can I get a little spending money too?

BRUNO removes his wallet, counts out a hundred bucks, hands it to **TOBIN**. **TOBIN** *starts to cry.*

BRUNO What's wrong?

TOBIN I'm such a fuckup.

BRUNO Tobin, come on, now, stop it.

TOBIN No, I am, Bruno. I'm a thirty-eight-year-old loser.

BRUNO You're the author of four highly acclaimed young adult novels.

TOBIN Yeah, why don't we italicize the "young adult" part for all my former classmates at Iowa! I wanted to be Vonnegut or Updike, and I turned out to be Louise Marie Alcott! I'm being published in the same genre as *Little House on the* fucking *Prairie*!

BRUNO Louisa *May* Alcott. And she wrote *Little Women*! Laura Ingalls Wilder wrote *Little House on the Prairie*!

TOBIN What's the difference?

BRUNO Tobin, I happen to think your novels are heads and shoulders above a lot of the *adult* books out there. No one captures voices like you. And fuck you, I *like* the *Little House on the Prairie* series! Laura Ingalls Wilder fucking rocks! Besides, we could have published *The Metal Children* as an adult book. Scribner was begging for it. *You* wanted to do it as a YA. You should be fucking *proud* of your career.

TOBIN My apartment's a mess. I can barely pay my rent. I have fucking hemorrhoids. My wife left me. Why did she leave me, Bruno?

BRUNO She fell in love with her editor. It happens.

TOBIN I miss her so much . . . Do you think she'd come back to me? If I started working out or something?

BRUNO Tobin, you look fine. I'm sure Miranda's leaving had a lot more to do with, well, other matters.

TOBIN But she could come back. It's possible, right?

BRUNO I suppose anything's possible. Stop crying now.

TOBIN *stops.*

BRUNO Do you really have hemorrhoids?

TOBIN Yes.

BRUNO Have you seen anyone about it?

TOBIN No. But I bought some Tucks.

BRUNO If they don't go away, promise me you'll see someone, okay?

TOBIN *nods.*

BRUNO Okay, I'm gonna go. *(gathering the video equipment)* I'll call you later with the car information.
TOBIN Hey, can I have that letter, the one from the teacher?

BRUNO *produces the letter, hands it to* TOBIN.

BRUNO You're a great writer, Tobin. I believe in you . . . We'll talk later, okay?

TOBIN *nods.* BRUNO *exits with his attaché case and video equipment. After the front door is closed,* TOBIN *removes the letter from the envelope, starts to read it as lights fade.*

SCENE 2

Five days later. A motel room in Midlothia, a small town in the American heartland.

A full-size bed and cheap headboard. A bedside stand with a digital clock radio. Blank baby-blue walls. A small round table with a chair. A door leading to a bathroom.

TOBIN *is standing in the middle of the room, staring at the wall, on which someone has spray-painted* GONE FOR NOW *in large, crude red letters.* TOBIN *is dressed in jeans and a T-shirt. He looks better but just barely. He holds a gym bag, and there is a suit bag lying across the bed.* EDITH, *a middle-aged woman, is standing behind him. She is run-down but possesses an inherent sweetness. She wears jeans and a cotton shirt that boasts the name of the motel. She holds fresh bedding.*

TOBIN You have no idea who did it?

EDITH Well, there was a pickup truck roaming around earlier. I think it was one of the Yeager boys, but he was wearing a mask.

TOBIN A mask.

EDITH Yeah, I'm almost certain it was Porky Pig.

TOBIN Do you think he wrote that on the wall?

She starts to strip the bed, which has soiled footprints on the comforter.

EDITH I guess it's possible. I mean, I have a clear view of your
     unit from the office, but they could've snuck in when I was
     restocking the candy machine. My niece was supposed to
     be watching the front desk, but I have no idea where she
     is. The sheriff said he'd be sending a car by . . . Is there
     anything I can do for you? Unfortunately I can't offer you a
     hot meal, but our vending options are quite good if I do say
     so myself.

TOBIN I'm fine, thanks.

EDITH (*remaking the bed*) So everyone's talking about the big
     meeting tomorrow. There were flyers hanging at the post
     office, and people were just buzzing at the supermarket.
     They even advertised it on the marquee at the high school.
     You must be *so* excited. I heard there's going to be reporters
     there and everything. Jerry Flagg from the pie shop said
     someone from *The New York Times* is flying in.

TOBIN Really.

EDITH Yeah, no kidding. Jerry never lies. And his pies are quite
     delicious.

TOBIN sets his things down, sits on the foot of the bed.

EDITH Well, you must be exhausted. Though the drive is quite
     scenic.

TOBIN Yeah, I took particular note of the nuclear power plant theme. I counted at least three pairs of apocalyptic chimneys billowing ominously stagnant disaster clouds.

EDITH I was actually referring to the hills.

TOBIN The hills were very nice. A little treacherous at times, but nice.

EDITH I guess it's true that we've had more than a few cars drive into the ravine. My niece likes to go down there and pick at the wreckage. I keep telling her it's none of her business, but she's at that age.

TOBIN How old is she?

EDITH Vera just turned sixteen. She's a junior at Midlothia Memorial.

TOBIN So she's aware of the controversy.

EDITH Principal Crowley himself pulled your book out of her hand while she was eating lunch in the cafeteria. It made her terribly upset. (*referring to the wall*) I wish I could offer you another room, but unfortunately we're all booked up because of the big meeting tomorrow.

TOBIN I'll be fine, thanks. (*referring to the wall*) What do you think it means?

EDITH *produces a hardcover copy of* The Metal Children *seemingly from out of nowhere.*

EDITH (*finding the page*) Page seventy-nine: "It was Shauna, all right. Same curly long hair. Same Joy Division concert T-shirt she wore every Tuesday with the loose neck and frayed shoulders. Same big, sad UFO eyes and death metal mouth. Same *Will someone please save me?* expression on her face. Same too-tight Gloria Vanderbilts and beat-to-shit Doc Martens. And on the base of the statue, in brilliant brass, the words 'Gone for now' were etched in perfect capital letters, as if old Mrs. Denton, the honors English teacher herself, was there just to make sure the words were right. 'Gone for now.' But where did Shauna go?" (*she closes the book*) Doesn't that ring a bell?

TOBIN I wrote it when I was twenty-six. After a while you forget the details.

EDITH I guess that's the nice thing about having it in a book. You can always open it back up . . . (*offering the book and producing a Sharpie*) Anyway, would you do me the honor, Mr. Falmouth?

He nods, accepts the book, leafs through to the title page, writes.

EDITH To Edith. No need to date it . . . When I heard about the controversy, I just had to read it. Unfortunately the local Barnes and Noble isn't carrying it anymore. The manager said they sold them all, but Jan Staley, who runs concessions at the Little League, told me that the church group bought them all and had them put in the vault.

TOBIN What church group?

EDITH The GCC. There's a pretty big chapter here in Midlothia.

TOBIN *has no idea what she's talking about.*

EDITH The Good Church of Christ. They mostly organize relief work and bowling nights, but your book seemed to really ruffle their feathers. I've never seen them get so active. Their office is over on Glavine Street.

TOBIN Is that where the infamous vault is?

EDITH I believe so, yes. And I understand it's quite a large vault at that. One hundred and forty cubic feet if I'm not mistaken. I got my copy from the Internet . . . I must say I got quite emotional while reading your book, Mr. Falmouth, which is fairly unusual for me with regard to artistic matters. I also got very angry for a moment or two. So much so that I actually shouted *Why? Why?* After I finished it, I immediately started over and read it again. And I'm actually rereading it a third time. I'm on page one hundred and seventeen, to be exact. That poor, poor Meredith Miller.

He hands her the book, exits to the bathroom. She reads the inscription, smiles, then closes it.

EDITH The women in my knitting circle read it too. Bev Newton and Phyllis Barinowski are just over the moon about it. They're the ones who started the Internet blog. But Roberta Cupp is pretty upset. She wrote a letter to the paper calling you a child pornographer. And boy, did that cause a stir. Several people wrote in that they agreed with her, but there were quite a few letters saying that you're not a child pornographer at all, but a messenger of difficult truths, and that to deprive children of these truths is to condescend to them.

She is drawn to his travel bag, almost snoops when TOBIN *reenters.*

TOBIN And what do you think?

EDITH Well, Mr. Falmouth, in one scene in particular you wrote very vividly about a young lady's genitalia. And while it was certainly a little shocking, I thought it was quite essential to the story. But what that poor girl does to herself in the final scene . . . She uses her father's hunting knife . . .

TOBIN We live in an ugly world.

EDITH Roberta Cupp started a pamphlet too.

She produces a pamphlet, hands it to him.

TOBIN *Kill This Book.* That's subtle.

EDITH Yeah, Roberta Cupp can get quite angry about things. She runs a self-defense class at the YMCA that incorporates a spatial skills workshop and Zen Budokai Jujitsu.

TOBIN Why do you have a pamphlet?

EDITH Because she left a stack of them for me to put on the counter in the office. I mostly use them for scrap paper.

The sound of a car parking. EDITH *pulls aside the curtain.*

EDITH Looks like they sent a squad car after all . . . Oh, it's Dave Tidwell! He's a world-class dart thrower and a passionate taxidermist. (*she lets the curtain fall*) Well, Mr. Falmouth, I suppose I should leave you alone. Just dial zero if you need anything. Would you like a wake-up call?

TOBIN No, thanks.

EDITH Okay, then. Good luck tomorrow. It's so nice to finally meet you.

TOBIN You too.

She exits. Headlights pan across his window. The sound of walkie-talkie static. The walkie-talkie fades. He sits on the bed, takes out a pot terrarium, removes papers, starts to roll a joint.

The phone rings twice. A knock on the door. He hides the pot. Another knock.

VOICE Mr. Falmouth?

TOBIN *opens the door to reveal a man in his mid-thirties. He is white, semiconservatively dressed in a blazer, jeans, and a tie.*

MAN Are you Tobin Falmouth?

TOBIN That would be me, yeah.

MAN (*offering his hand*) I'm Stacey Kinsella. The English teacher from Midlothia Memorial . . . I wrote you the letter . . . about your book *The Metal Children*?

TOBIN (*shocked it's a man*) Oh, the *letter*, right. Hi.

STACEY (*shaking hands*) It's so nice to finally meet you.

TOBIN You too.

STACEY May I come in?

TOBIN Sure, sure.

STACEY *enters, closes the door.*

STACEY So you made it. You're actually here.

TOBIN I am. I'm here.

STACEY By the way, is that your big black SUV with the Jersey plates?

TOBIN Yeah, why?

STACEY Well, don't kill the messenger, but they egged it. They egged my car too. They also broke three of my windows, slashed my tires, and defecated in the backseat. They painted stuff on my house too.

TOBIN What did they paint on your house?

STACEY The same thing that's on your wall there. Plus "Die, Artfag Die!" in big red letters. They painted some shapes too.

TOBIN What shapes?

STACEY Well, there was an oddly drawn cross. And a triangle with an *X* through it. And this other arrangement that I think is supposed to be some sort of primate sodomizing an adolescent Jesus of Nazareth. I don't mean to invade your privacy, Mr. Falmouth, I just . . . well, I had nowhere else to go. If it isn't too much trouble, would you mind if I stayed with you for a few hours? With that squad car out there I'd feel a lot safer.

TOBIN If your tires were slashed, how did you get here?

STACEY I walked. It's only a few miles. If you cut through the woods . . . In any event, I'm really glad you made it. My students are going to be *so* excited. The girls just love you. The boys too. But the *girls*. Your book means so much to them, Mr. Falmouth.

From his gym bag, TOBIN *produces a bottle of bourbon.*

TOBIN Bourbon?

STACEY Oh, no, thanks.

TOBIN Don't drink?

STACEY No, I just . . . Midlothia's sort of a dry town. Well, unofficially dry.

The sound of squealing tires from the parking lot. STACEY *crosses to the curtains, peeks through a crack, closes them, turns back.* TOBIN *puts the bourbon back in his bag.*

STACEY So I very much liked your follow-up to *The Metal Children. Rock Elm.* The plans of an at-large teen serial killer mysteriously carved into the bark of local elm trees. Pretty intense stuff. I mentioned the possibility of bringing *Rock Elm* into the curriculum as a companion piece to *The Metal Children*, but a parent who sits on the committee that helps choose the books felt you had pushed the envelope a bit much for the young adult market. I disagreed, of course.

TOBIN I actually don't consider the things I write young adult.

STACEY But your stuff is so great for teens.

TOBIN The young adult market is a ghetto, Stacey.

STACEY Oh? How so?

TOBIN You get no newspaper coverage. Book tours are out of the question. Print runs are barely a few thousand copies, and it's basically a literary miracle if your publisher goes back to press. You're essentially relegated to dank library basements and rickety classroom shelves. And while I appreciate progressive librarians and teachers like yourself, as an author you can't help but feel that your audience is force-fed.

STACEY (*hurt*) Force-fed?

TOBIN I'm sorry. I don't mean to sound cynical. My attitude clearly sucks. I shouldn't be dumping all that on you. Things have been a little, well, rough lately.

STACEY Anything you want to talk about?

TOBIN Well, for starters I'm nine months late on my latest book, I can't seem to pay my rent, and my wife recently left me.

STACEY I'm sorry to hear that . . . How long were you married?

TOBIN Seven years. We met at Iowa and moved to New York after we graduated.

STACEY Is she a writer too?

TOBIN She is, yes.

STACEY Teen fiction?

TOBIN She writes literary mystery novels for adults. Her name is Miranda McCloud.

STACEY You were married to Miranda McCloud? I've read all four of her books in the Sadie Chase series. *Calypso Nights* is absolutely riveting! She's a genius!

TOBIN Well, currently there's one less genius in my life because she left me. For another man.

STACEY I'm sorry . . . Who's the other man? If you don't mind me asking.

TOBIN Her editor.

STACEY Hmmm.

TOBIN Yeah.

STACEY Older?

TOBIN Younger, actually. Younger, richer, handsomer . . . thinner . . . I think I might have that drink now.

He takes out the bourbon from his bag again, opens the bourbon, drinks.

STACEY Do you and Miranda have kids?

TOBIN No. Why do you ask?

STACEY Oh, no reason. It's just that you write about them so insightfully.

TOBIN We were all young once.

STACEY True.

TOBIN Those years never leave us.

STACEY They certainly don't, do they?

TOBIN *drinks, offers the bottle.*

STACEY Oh, what the hey.

TOBIN *pours some bourbon into a plastic motel cup on the table, passes it to* STACEY.

TOBIN To the children.
STACEY To *The Metal Children.*
TOBIN To *The Metal Children.*

STACEY *takes a nip, swallows, does his best to maintain good drinking composure.*

The phone rings. TOBIN *answers it.*

TOBIN Hello? . . . (*looks at the phone, puts it back to his ear*) Hello? . . .

He hangs up.

STACEY Who was it?
TOBIN It was a vacuum cleaner.
STACEY A vacuum cleaner. Well, that's curious.
TOBIN *Shshshshs* . . . Listen . . .

They listen intently. Suddenly a distinct thump on the front door and then squealing tires. TOBIN *crosses toward the door.*

STACEY Wait!!! Take this!!!

TOBIN That's a hunting knife, Stacey . . . Why do you have a hunting knife?

A knock on the door. TOBIN *takes the knife.*

VOICE Mr. Falmouth, it's me . . . Edith Dundee from the motel office.

TOBIN *hides the hunting knife, opens the door.* EDITH *is standing there, holding a damp loaf of meat.*

EDITH It appears you've been hammed, Mr. Falmouth . . . Hello, Mr. Kinsella.

STACEY Hello, Edith.

EDITH I'm so sorry. Officer Tidwell came by the office to say hello when I saw that truck again. Officer Tidwell went after whoever it was.

They all stare at the loaf of meat.

EDITH (*to* TOBIN, *holding up the ham*) In your book they throw large chunks of ham through Meredith Miller's bedroom window, and she brings it to school and offers it to her classmates in the cafeteria line.

STACEY Actually in the novel it's tins of Spam, Edith. I believe that's a headcheese.

TOBIN What's a headcheese?

STACEY A jellied loaf or sausage made from chopped and

boiled parts of the feet, head, and sometimes the tongue and heart of an animal, usually a hog. I've often used it as a flavorful blue cheese companion for my Dijon vinaigrette dressing.

EDITH What do you think it means?

STACEY I assume it represents the same thing it did in Mr. Falmouth's novel: the inviolable fetus. In the abstract, of course. (*to* TOBIN) Please correct me if I'm wrong.

TOBIN Sounds good to me.

STACEY (*to* EDITH, *referring to the headcheese*) Want me to take that?

She hands it to him.

STACEY How's your niece, Edith?

EDITH Vera's fine, thanks. At the moment she's supposed to be covering the front desk. And I have no idea why she just bleached her hair. (*to* TOBIN) My niece has this beautiful head of dark curly hair.

STACEY It's what Meredith Miller does in the novel. After the whole town finds out that she's pregnant, she bleaches her hair.

EDITH That's right, she does bleach her hair, doesn't she? What do you suppose that means?

The phone rings again. TOBIN *answers the phone, listens, hangs up. He and* STACEY *share a look.*

EDITH What's the matter?

STACEY Edith, is there a vacuum cleaner on the premises?

EDITH Of course there is. We just got a new Eureka Sanitaire S677A with eight carpet positions and a quick-clean Vibra. Has there been some sort of a spill?

TOBIN No, no spill.

STACEY We were just curious.

EDITH (*getting nervous*) Well, just let me know if you need it. I'm going to go call the sheriff's office.

She exits.

TOBIN So are your students getting pregnant?

STACEY I think some of them might be, yes.

TOBIN Because of the book?

STACEY I don't think I can answer that, Mr. Falmouth.

TOBIN Because you don't know or because you don't want to?

STACEY Because it's not that simple. I will say that I think a lot of the young women in this community feel crushingly insignificant. Somehow your book has tapped into something that they're longing for.

TOBIN What, motherhood?

STACEY I'd call it something like a singular, unadulterated purpose. In your novel they are glorified for it.

TOBIN Stacey, they *disappear*.

STACEY And then they are bronzed and made permanent. And in the final chapter, at the feet of all those statues, in a moonlit cornfield, Meredith Miller aborts her own fetus

with her father's hunting knife. And all of those girls from
that made-up town in Iowa are mythologized into cultural
martyrdom . . .

The sound of rain swells.

TOBIN Oh, great. Now it's raining.
STACEY Yeah, I worry about the kids.
TOBIN Why?
STACEY They like hanging out over at the old limestone quarry.
When it rains, things can get pretty slippery.

TOBIN *drinks, offers* **STACEY** *the bottle again.* **STACEY** *nods, sets the*
headcheese on the table. **TOBIN** *pours bourbon into his cup, hands*
it to him. They drink.

STACEY So what are you planning on saying in front of the
school board tomorrow?
TOBIN To be honest, I'm not exactly sure yet.
STACEY Well, whatever it is, I can guarantee that Otto Hurley
will be interested.
TOBIN Who's Otto Hurley?
STACEY The chair of the school board. He owns a cement
company and has a rather booming voice. But don't be
intimidated. The best thing to do is stand your ground.
Even if the Pork Patrol starts pressing in on you.
TOBIN What's the Pork Patrol?
STACEY Just some boys from school who harass people.

They're small-minded bullies, but they think of themselves as community regulators. They believe community "pork" is bad for community "health." One of them is quite accomplished with nunchackus. They wear Porky Pig masks and metal baseball cleats.

TOBIN Jesus. Where the hell am I?

STACEY You're in Midlothia. Famous for its limestone, nuclear power, and the largest Black & Decker factory outlet in America.

TOBIN How did you wind up here?

STACEY I went to a small liberal arts college about thirty-five miles north. There was a vacancy in the English Department here, so I applied . . . I guess I thought I could do the most good by walking right into the mouth of the lion.

TOBIN And how did you manage to bring my book into the curriculum?

STACEY Former Superintendent Waldvogel is a very progressive man. I was blown away by the book. I passed it along to him, and he responded. When things about your book got inflammatory, the school board asked Perry to resign.

TOBIN Where is he now?

STACEY No one knows for sure. He hasn't been spotted in weeks. He put his house on the market, but no one will buy it. He has relatives in Spokane, Washington. My guess is that he went there.

TOBIN You two were close.

STACEY Perry and I were close, yes.

TOBIN Like *close* close?

STACEY That's certainly one way of putting it.

Suddenly the sound of a cell phone. STACEY *reaches into the pocket of his blazer, removes a cell phone.*

STACEY Excuse me.

He answers the phone.

STACEY Hello? . . . Hello, Brian . . . Uh-huh . . . Uh-huh . . . Oh, dear . . . Well I'll get there as soon as I can.

He hangs up.

TOBIN Something wrong?

STACEY That was one of my students. He just told me that they set my lawn on fire.

TOBIN But it's raining.

STACEY They have very advanced techniques, Mr. Falmouth . . . May I borrow your truck?

TOBIN *hesitates, then hands him the keys.*

STACEY Thank you . . . I'm not drunk, am I?

TOBIN I don't know, Stacey. Do you feel drunk?

STACEY I don't think so. Do I look okay?

TOBIN You look fine.

STACEY I'm really glad you're here. This really is important, what's happening.

TOBIN nods. STACEY continues to stand there.

TOBIN What's wrong?

STACEY May I have my knife back, please?

TOBIN gives him the knife.

STACEY Thank you, Mr. Falmouth.

TOBIN Sure, Stacey. Drive safe.

STACEY nods, thaws, exits. TOBIN sits in silence for a moment, grabs the phone, dials.

TOBIN (*into phone*) Miranda, hey, it's me . . . Um, I'm in this place called Midlothia, where they just banned my book. I'm at the Blue Moon Motel, to be exact . . . It's about ten-thirty, and it's raining . . . I just wanted to let you know that I miss you . . . (*he starts to cry, makes himself stop*) I know I promised I wouldn't call . . . Anyway, the number here is six-one-one, nine-two-one, four-five-nine-four. I'm in room seven . . . Okay then.

He hangs up, crosses to the bathroom, exits.

Moments later a young woman enters with a can of spray paint.
She is sixteen, very pretty, with blond hair. She wears army fatigue
pants and combat boots, and she is wet from the rain. One of her
hands is painted gold. She stands on the bed and begins spray-
painting over the red GONE FOR NOW *words in a shade of blue*
that almost matches the color on the wall. She works quickly.

TOBIN *enters from the bathroom.*

TOBIN Can I help you?

She steps down from the bed.

TOBIN It's comforting to know that when you travel far
    distances, your motel room might be broken into at any
    possible moment.
GIRL I saw your truck pull out of the lot. I thought you were
    in it. I was trying to be discreet.
TOBIN What are you doing?
GIRL Covering up those words.
TOBIN Why the disdain for the words?
GIRL Because they represent a fascistic, bigoted element of this
    community. And in my opinion, considering the source
    material, it's a pretty dismal attempt at irony. I'm Vera.
TOBIN You're Edith's niece. I assume you're involved with the
    petition, and you just bleached your hair. You're supposed
    to be watching the front desk.

VERA I've got more important things on my plate right now.
And I'm not just involved with the petition, I started it.

TOBIN Oh. Well, in that case you could've just knocked on the door.

Pause.

VERA You look different from your author photo.

TOBIN Sorry if I disappoint.

VERA It's not disappointing. Just different.

TOBIN (*referring to the wall*) Well, don't let me stop you.

She steps back onto the bed, continues spray-painting.

TOBIN So how many names do you have on the petition now?

VERA Seven hundred and sixteen.

TOBIN How many students are there?

VERA Well, there are only five hundred and six at Midlothia
Memorial, but our website has been getting quite a few hits.

TOBIN I didn't know there was a website.

VERA Meredith Miller dot com. We've posted student quotes,
art inspired by the First Amendment, and excerpted
selections from the novel. There's also a flash animation
sequence of Meredith Miller's final action with her father's
hunting knife. This artist from Canada submitted it.
Anatomically-speaking, it's pretty convincing.

TOBIN I'll have to check it out.

VERA We'd love to get a quote from you at some point.

TOBIN Buy low, sell high.

Beat.

TOBIN So are the students for or against it?

VERA It's about sixty-forty.

TOBIN And the teachers?

VERA More like seventy-thirty.

TOBIN Seventy in favor?

VERA Against. The janitors like it, though. One of them was carrying a copy around in his back pocket. But then he got fired.

The phone rings. TOBIN *answers it quickly.*

TOBIN (*into phone*) Miranda? . . . Hello? . . .

He listens for a moment and then hangs up.

VERA Who was it?

TOBIN It would appear that a certain persistent vacuum cleaner has something important to say to me.

VERA In your book, before each girl disappears, the phone rings, and when she answers, the only thing on the other end is the sound of a vacuum cleaner. Mr. Kinsella says that even though you don't explain it in an explicit manner, the vacuum cleaner sound is a cultural comment on the SU-507 180-watt Crown Suction Unit, the most heavily utilized abortion apparatus currently available in the U.S. Is that true?

TOBIN Um, sure . . . Who do you think's actually *running* that vacuum cleaner?

VERA The one from the novel?

TOBIN The one I just heard through the phone.

VERA My guess is that it's either the Christians or the Pork Patrol.

A coded knock on the door. VERA *quickly crosses to the door, opens it.* COOPER, VERA*'s classmate, stands in the entrance. She is similarly dressed, a messenger bag slung around her shoulder.*

COOPER (*to* VERA) Is that him?

VERA Mr. Falmouth, this is Cooper.

TOBIN Hi, Cooper.

COOPER (*almost losing it*) Oh my God oh my God oh my God oh my God oh my God oh my God—

VERA You got the paint?

COOPER *removes three cans of spray paint from her messenger bag, hands them to* VERA.

COOPER (*to* VERA) They tagged the water tower.

VERA Fucking pigs! (*to* COOPER) You better get back out there.

COOPER *approaches* TOBIN, *prostrates herself, hugs him around the knees.*

COOPER It was an honor to meet you. Mr. Falmouth.

TOBIN You too, Cooper.

COOPER *exits.* VERA *sits on the bed. After a short silence:*

VERA Who's Miranda?

TOBIN Miranda's my wife. Well, ex-wife.

VERA Is she in trouble or something?

TOBIN No, why?

VERA You just seemed really desperate when you answered the phone.

TOBIN By desperate you mean pathetic.

VERA Pathetic implies seeking pity. Desperation deals more with pure hopelessness. It's a fine line.

TOBIN You don't see me as someone seeking pity?

VERA I don't see you seeking much of anything.

TOBIN . . . Why is your hand gold?

VERA It's something my friends and I do in honor of your book. We started out painting our index fingers in English class.

TOBIN Mr. Kinsella obviously didn't mind.

VERA He gave us money for the body paint. A few of us tried it in twentieth-century American history. And then in chem lab. A week later we did two fingers, and ten of us brought it into gym class. It's been a finger a week after that. Three days ago thirty-five of us bleached our hair.

TOBIN . . . So can I ask you a question?

VERA Sure.

TOBIN How many of your bleached-blond friends are pregnant?

VERA A few, why?

TOBIN Are they trying to get pregnant?

VERA Well, after the GCC got their way, Midlothia Memorial ceased the free condom program, so you figure that has something to do with it. But there is a kind of vision being executed, I will admit to that.

TOBIN What kind of a vision?

VERA The kind of vision where you close your eyes and see things.

TOBIN That's a little oblique.

VERA What my friends and I are up to has nothing to do with being oblique. If anything, we're too direct . . . Your book woke a lot of people up, Mr. Falmouth.

TOBIN And here I thought it was on the verge of going out of print.

VERA The novelist might be the only true cultural revolutionary left in America.

TOBIN Who said that?

VERA I did.

TOBIN And you grew up in a roadside motel?

VERA Joan of Arc grew up on a peasant farm.

TOBIN Yeah, she also heard voices.

VERA I hear cars go by on the highway. And when I close my eyes, sometimes I do see things.

TOBIN Define "cultural revolutionary."

VERA A revolutionary is somebody committed to a political or social movement. So a *cultural* revolutionary wreaks his or her havoc through art, music, literature, and related intellectual activities. With prose, the novelist grapples with the purity of thought more than anyone else. Good fiction teaches a reader how to develop the instrument that becomes the voice in his or her head. The words are absorbed purely, without music or three-dimensional imagery. As a reader you construct the world of the book *with* the author. You're in essence a performer. A creationist. That's why they're so afraid out there. And I'm not just talking about Midlothia, Mr. Falmouth. I'm talking about America. The novel gets at your thought ten times more powerfully than the stuff on TV. In every novel there lurks a sweet invisible monster that waits for the reader to fall asleep. And then with its obovoid toddler's mouth and panda-bear eyes this monster kneels down at said reader's bedside and whispers all the unbearable truths that commodified pharmaceuticals, network television, and Swanson microwave dinners try and cover up. And this will ultimately advance the culture. Your book is like intellectual anthrax.

TOBIN Wouldn't that make me a terrorist?

VERA One girl's terrorist is another girl's revolutionary.

TOBIN *How* old are you?

VERA Old enough to know that we only have so much time on this earth, so why spend it half asleep with the television on?

TOBIN Where'd you learn all this stuff?

VERA Well, Mr. Kinsella's been a big help.

TOBIN It must be a great class.

VERA He talks to us like we're capable of having our own thoughts . . . Why are you looking at me like that?

TOBIN I'll ask you again. Are you and your friends trying to get pregnant?

VERA There's a boy at Midlothia Memorial. Let's call him Boy X because I have to protect his anonymity. Boy X has been selected by the movement because along with being a pretty nice guy who happens to respect women, he has an unusually high sperm count. He's our host donor. Currently fourteen of the girls who have bleached their hair are pregnant from his sperm.

TOBIN Jesus Christ.

VERA Jesus Christ has nothing to do with it. Jesus Christ was at best a skinny vegetarian social charmer with great hair and a penchant for magic tricks.

TOBIN Boy X. Lucky kid.

VERA Three of my sisters slept with him two days ago. We have an ovulation schedule. We use the First Response early result pregnancy test, and we are hopeful.

TOBIN Vera, do you have any idea what you girls are getting yourselves into?

VERA Would I be here right now if I didn't?

TOBIN Are you planning on keeping these babies?

VERA Yes.

TOBIN And who is going to parent them?

VERA My sisters and I.

TOBIN What about your futures?

VERA We're starting a community. In McCall, Idaho. There's a farmhouse and two acres of fertile land. We've put twenty percent down. A lawyer we met through the website is cosigning the mortgage for us.

TOBIN Where'd you get the money?

VERA From Meredith Miller T-shirts. We silk-screen them ourselves. They go for ten bucks each on the website. So far we've sold over two thousand of them, and we can't keep up with the back orders.

TOBIN But who's going to help you for the next nine months?

VERA We're capable young women, Mr. Falmouth. We'll help each other.

TOBIN But why get pregnant?

VERA Because we can. Existentially speaking, aside from suicide, it's the most meaningful choice a young woman can make. We control our own fate. Not parents or priests or politicians. Not coaches or teachers of textbooks preapproved by the educational oligarchy. Not middle-aged men with prostate problems and hairy ears. We get pregnant, our community automatically exiles us, our parents disown us. No man wants to be with a single teen mother. We take control of our own destiny. Whether you like it or not, your novel showed us that, Mr. Falmouth. (*checking her watch*) Now we only have about thirty minutes before my aunt starts making rounds of the units. Do you have any sexually transmitted diseases?

TOBIN No. Why?

VERA Well, I'm ovulating and actually quite excited about the prospect of the creator of our great text being my host. There's powerful poetry at play. You're not sterile, are you?

She takes her shirt off, her pants.

VERA Your fertility is sort of paramount to this actually happening, Mr. Falmouth.

TOBIN I'm totally not sterile.

In her bra and panties, she turns the covers down.

TOBIN Do you have a dad?

VERA I had a dad. And then I didn't have a dad.

TOBIN Oh. Do you have a mom?

VERA They drove into the ravine when I was two. In a red '74 Volkswagen Bug. They both died on impact.

TOBIN They drove into the ravine on purpose?

VERA Apparently the car was packed and they were running away.

TOBIN Where were they going?

VERA No one knows.

TOBIN Where were you?

VERA They left me with my aunt.

TOBIN Here at the motel?

VERA At the Blue Moon Motel, yep.

TOBIN And she's raised you on her own?

VERA Mr. Falmouth, if what you're asking is whether or not there's some large, broad-shouldered father-figure type lurking about the premises, the answer is no. My aunt's never been married. I don't even think she's been laid in over thirty years, if at all. But just to be discreet, I might suggest locking the door.

TOBIN (*locking the door*) Um, so can I ask you another question?

VERA What?

TOBIN Are you a virgin?

VERA Would you like me to be a virgin?

TOBIN Yes.

VERA Then I'm a virgin.

He turns the light off. She starts to sing a song.

VERA (*singing*)
    In a new land we will gather
    And make the children safe and strong
    Break the chains made by our fathers
    Till the soil and sing our song
    Let our voices shake the treetops
    Press our bodies to the soil
    Meredith
    Meredith Miller
    Praise to her, forever loyal

He reaches out, touches her cheek. She stops singing, simply stares up at him as lights fade.

SCENE 3

The motel room. Middle of the night.

Darkness.

Moonlight from the window. TOBIN *is sleeping, alone.*

The door is quietly opened. A boy with a high-powered flashlight is standing in the entrance, half silhouetted. His face is covered with a Porky Pig mask. He wears metal baseball cleats and mans a large vacuum cleaner.

The BOY *shuts the door, turns the vacuum cleaner on, trains the flashlight on* TOBIN'*s face, produces a pair of nunchackus, and proceeds to knock the living shit out of him, driving him into the bathroom.*

When TOBIN *is good and beaten, the* BOY IN THE PORKY PIG MASK *exits with the flashlight, leaving the vacuum cleaner on.*

End of Act I

ACT II

SCENE 1

The school board meeting, the auditorium at Midlothia Memorial High School. Seated at a long convention table, from left to right, are TAMI LAKE, *sixteen,* VERA DUNDEE, *all visible flesh painted gold,* TOBIN, *with two black eyes, looking a little worse for wear, and* ROBERTA CUPP, *mid-forties, righteous and repressed, but ready to blow. There is an empty chair between* TOBIN *and* ROBERTA CUPP *where* STACEY KINSELLA *is supposed to be seated, and we know this because in front of each person is a name place card. Set on the table are two pitchers of ice water. A glass has been placed in front of each person. Next to the table is a lectern.*

The proceedings are being led by OTTO HURLEY. *He has a deep, booming voice.*

OTTO Good evening, everyone. As you know, I'm Otto Hurley, the chair of the Midlothia County school board. Thank you for coming to what promises to be an illuminating special assembly. Before we begin, I want to extend hearty gratitude to the faculty and staff of Midlothia Memorial High School for lending us their spacious auditorium. I'm afraid our normal meeting place at the Horace Ciderhoff Community Center wouldn't be able to hold tonight's audience, as many of you have come from far and wide.

We're gathered here to discuss the recent events surrounding the young adult novel *The Metal Children*, written by one Tobin Foulmouth, who happens to be with us this evening. It's nice to finally put a face to a name. Welcome, Mr. Foulmouth.

As many of you know, this novel has inspired considerable controversy due to what a strong contingent in the community believes to be salacious, immoral content, content that many in our midst believe glorifies premarital sex, teen pregnancy, and a questionable young woman's grisly, self-inflicted abortion and suicide involving a six-inch serrated hunting knife.

SEVERAL YOUNG FEMALE VOICES FROM OFFSTAGE: MEREDITH MILLER LIVES FOREVER!

VERA DUNDEE *thrusts a power fist into the air.*

OTTO Quiet, please . . .

The auditorium hushes.

OTTO Thank you. At our last meeting, Mr. Stacey Kinsella, the chair of the English Department at Midlothia Memorial, motioned that copies of *The Metal Children* were seized—or banned, as I've recently gleaned to be the common phrasing—without following proper procedure. Mr. Kinsella also vehemently defended the book, citing its quote, unquote "important social and cultural message" and articulating some additional cockamamie about how works of literature can act as a preventative intellectual vaccine for readers.

The following day it was brought to my attention by former Superintendent Waldvogel that our rash act of literary confiscation was indeed inappropriate, and for that I owe the community an apology. There are procedures set in place, and it is important that we follow them. It won't happen again, I assure you.

As many of you know, due to unknown reasons, Mr. Waldvogel has since resigned—quite suddenly, I might add—and I know I speak for many when I say that we are perhaps as confused as we are saddened by this flight from such a valued station in our community.

In our defense, I believe that my fellow board members and I took a desperate measure to eradicate what we felt to be a virulent element that was threatening to pollute the minds of our young people. All copies of the said title are currently being held in a sealed vault that our good friends at the Good Church of Christ have been kind enough to provide, and it has yet to be determined whether or not the forty-some copies of the book will be restored to the curriculum. Hopefully the outcome of this meeting will help us make that determination.

Seated before you are four . . . well, *three* members of the Midlothia community as well as our guest from New York City. All . . . *four* panelists have various opinions of and relationships to the book in question. Our panelists are:

Tami Lake, a junior currently enrolled at Midlothia Memorial; Vera Dundee, one of her classmates, who is obviously confused about what month we're in—the last time I checked, Halloween was at the end of October, Vera—and as I said just moments ago, also with us this evening is the author of *The Metal Children*, Tobin Foulmouth—

TOBIN Um, it's *Falmouth*, actually. First syllable "fal," as in the season between September and November, second syllable "mouth," pronounced "myth." Like the myth of Sisyphus or the myth of Hercules. Falmouth.

OTTO I mean Falmouth. Glad you could make it to Midlothia, friend.

TOBIN Glad to be here.

OTTO And the person intended to be seated beside our guest is the head of the Midlothia Memorial English Department, Stacey Kinsella—does anybody actually know where Mr. Kinsella is?

No answer.

OTTO Well, hopefully he'll make an appearance. As I see it, he's the one responsible for this whole mess. And finally, seated on the other side of Mr. Falmouth is Roberta Cupp, and many of you in the community know Roberta, I'm sure. Hello, Roberta.

ROBERTA Hello, Otto.

OTTO Each member of the panel will have a minute or two to share their thoughts and feelings regarding the novel, and after everyone has spoken, we will open it up to the floor for your welcome response. The goal here is to engage in a dialogue, not a diatribe. Let's keep that in mind, please. Tami?

TAMI LAKE *pushes away from the table, approaches the lectern with a piece of paper. She takes a deep breath, begins speaking.*

TAMI According to the book of Genesis, God is involved in the creation of every living thing. You see a hawk in the sky. God made it. A cow grazing in a distant field. God made it. A puppy nursing. God made it. And more specifically, God is involved in the creation of all human beings. Mother. Father. The union of love. Our Heavenly Father blesses us with the miracle of procreation. He gives us the possibility of what is perhaps our greatest gift for being alive: child.

In his book *The Metal Children*, by having young girls get pregnant and then mythologized with brass sculptures, Tobin Falmouth is attempting to glorify teen pregnancy, premarital sex, and antisocial behavior. These are not qualities high school students should be exposed to in preparing for college and life in general. The main character, Meredith Miller, a selfish, godless outcast, performs a horrible deed at the feet of the statues of her peers, preventing the life of her unborn child with her father's six-inch serrated hunting knife. Meredith Miller murders her baby in a cornfield. This is disgusting, not to mention illegal.

The Sixth Commandment: Thou. Shalt. Not. Kill.

I know I represent many of the Christian faith in this community when I say that this book should be kept not only out of the classroom but also away from shopping malls, convention centers, bookmobiles, chain and private bookselling operations (i.e., Barnes & Noble and Black Pond Books on Clancy Street), and all public libraries. Let's keep *The Metal Children* out of our homes and away from our community. Thank you.

A smattering of applause. She sits down, pours water, drinks.

OTTO Thank you, Tami. In light of the situation, as a fellow Christian I commend your courage and fortitude. Next up is Vera Dundee. As we know, Vera is the young lady responsible for starting the student petition in support of the book. She's also done something quite interesting with her makeup this evening, and I assume there will be an explanation. Vera?

VERA *takes the lectern.*

SEVERAL YOUNG FEMALE VOICES FROM OFFSTAGE:
MEREDITH MILLER LIVES FOREVER!!! WE
LOVE YOU, MEREDITH!!! WOO-WOO-WOO!!!
MEREDITH MILLER DOT-COM!!!

OTTO Ladies, if you can't control yourselves, I'm going to have to have you removed from the auditorium. Sheriff Heffner, would you please see to any more outbursts? . . . Whenever you're ready, Vera.

VERA Thank you, Mr. Hurley. Before I begin, I just have to say that when one is looking to illustrate moral absolutes, it's easy to turn to scripture, a piece of literature that has been translated so many times by so many cultures that some scholars believe it to be the single most mutilated text in the history of the known world. Thank you, Tami, for helping to further facilitate what the Christian Coalition, Toby Keith, Rupert Murdoch, and Fox News have been campaigning so hard for in recent years: to secure our country's swift and relentless return to the Dark Ages.

TAMI You're tainted.

VERA I'll begin now. (*reading from a piece of paper*) Perhaps art's greatest responsibility in a democracy is to hold a mirror up. To his actors, Hamlet instructs the following:

Suit the action to the word, the word to the action, with this special observance, that you o'erstep not the modesty of nature: for anything so overdone is from the purpose of playing, whose end, both at the first and now, was and is, to hold as 'twere the mirror up to nature: to show virtue her own feature, scorn her own image, and the very age and body of the time his form and pressure.

[handwritten margin note: show things as they are, even named after thing]

As we learn from Shakespeare's great eponymous work, storytelling's function, whether it be spoken by the mouths of actors on a stage or discovered in the pages of books, is not to simply entertain and spread the mind-numbing analgesic that television and video games do so virally, but to show us who we are and what is wrong with the world around us; to help us understand the complexity and confounding realities of what it means to be human. The function of great literary works is not only to amuse but to shake the reader, to present the truth, no matter how grisly or unbearable.

Each year, almost one million teenage American women—ten percent of all women aged fifteen to nineteen—become pregnant. Fifty-six percent of these pregnancies result in births. Thirty percent in abortions. Fourteen percent in miscarriages.

With *The Metal Children*, Mr. Falmouth takes the truth of these numbers and concocts a heart-stopping fable where twenty-three young women at a fictional high school in the American heartland are not only getting pregnant but also inexplicably disappearing. Meredith Miller, the heroine of his beautiful novel, martyrs herself and her fetus at the feet of all those statues that we've heard so much about these past weeks. Is this ending painful? Yes. Is it harrowing? Yes. Did I cry when I read it? Yes. Did it anger me? Yes. It also made me think about my life in a way that I hadn't in a very long time. What if I had sex without a condom and became pregnant? Would I have the child? Would I abort the fetus? Would I give it up for adoption? Would I leave town and never look back? And is the ending explained? Is it

Pain killing

carved up and served to its reader like a good Thanksgiving turkey? No. It is difficult and devastating—perhaps savage even—and is left up to the reader to interpret.

In my view, Mr. Falmouth's novel is a cutting but keenly observed commentary on the failure of a community to find solutions for its younger generation. After the deacon of the local church finds Meredith Miller lying dead in that cornfield, still clutching her father's hunting knife, he doesn't kneel down and pray for her soul or seek the sympathy in his heart; he slaps her. And that's how the book ends. The spiritual leader of Meredith Miller's community slaps her cold, dead face. And that's what's happening here in Midlothia. The school board, in conjunction with the Good Church of Christ and a gaggle of parents shrouded in cloaks of fear, is slapping not only the students from Mr. Kinsella's class who were so moved and inspired by *The Metal Children*, but every single one of us here tonight. To remove art from a culture is to name that culture dead! I'll say it again! To remove art from a culture is to name that culture dead!

In closing, I would like to explain why I am painted gold tonight. Thirty-nine students from Mr. Kinsella's Great Books class are currently standing in the Midlothia Memorial football field. Like me, they are all painted gold. They are all standing very still, I'd even say statuelike, and holding candles as a kind of vigil. After the assembly, I will join them to become the fortieth student. And I too will hold a candle and stand as still as I can. And we will remain standing across the fifty-yard line for three hours as a protest against the ridiculous and unfortunate confiscation of *The Metal Children*. And you're all welcome to come by and take in this vision of support for Mr. Falmouth's novel. It's a hundred and ninety-eight pages, and it will rock your world. Meredith Miller lives forever!

VERA *steps down from the lectern. Enormous cheers and hoots from her classmates and other young people.*

OTTO Roberta?

ROBERTA CUPP *approaches the lectern, holding the book.*

ROBERTA Thank you, Otto . . . Good evening, everyone.
   First and foremost, on behalf of the Good Church of Christ, I want to thank you all for coming out to this special assembly. I'm proud to represent an important voice in the community during such a trying time.
   Parents, teachers, librarians, coaches, civic leaders, I beseech you. The message contained within the pages of this book is not a good one. One of our jobs as community leaders is to find ways for our young people to connect with the world in positive ways, to help mentor them toward making sound moral choices as they approach adulthood.
   Unfortunately, our world is already polluted with depravity. One only has to turn on the evening news or simply type in a URL address on one's Web browser to

find oneself in the midst of unthinkable violence and pornography. Do I need to list such things? No. We all know they're there. I'd rather not do that kind of work tonight.

My question to everyone gathered here tonight is this: Why do we need more of the same negativity in our literature? Is it *necessary* to bring the grisly subjects of abortion, teen pregnancy, and sorcery into the classroom? When the world is already oversaturated with sex, drugs, war, and profanity, is this kind of material *really essential* to the methods of teaching our young people? In our *English classes*, no less? An important cog in our educational process that has the opportunity to teach poetry and beauty and the unities of the classics? I believe sensationalistic works such as *The Metal Children* are not essential, and I know I represent many gathered here tonight when I say Mr. Falmouth's book should be kept out of the hands of our young people. There are hundreds, even thousands, of challenging texts that don't traffic in decadence and social and spiritual depravity.

And regarding this petition: we must not succumb to the impulsive, uninformed passions of our young people. I would argue that though many who have signed this document are intelligent, well-meaning community youths, they know not the seeds of darkness that are sown in the pages of this book. They know not the stain this work will leave on their souls. Without question we must stand by the decision of our very capable school board. We have elected each member to their post for a reason, and we must support their informed, careful decision. I know I speak for many Christians in the Midlothian community and beyond when I say God is watching and He appreciates the good work you are doing. I passionately stand by the confiscation of this book and I think it is a wise decision to keep it far away from our classrooms. Praise God and bless the children. Thank you.

ROBERTA *returns to her seat.*

OTTO Thank you, Roberta. Nicely done.

Suddenly TAMI *takes center stage and performs the following choreographed number (*ROBERTA *may lip-synch some of the words throughout):*

TAMI CHILDREN!
    WOMB LIGHT!
    THE BREATH OF GOD!
    CHRIST DYING FOR OUR SINS!
    A MIRACLE!
    THE FEAST OF LIFE!
    OUR HEAVENLY FATHER!
    BLOWS POLLEN FROM HIS FINGERTIPS!
    AND BEFORE US!
    IS DELIVERED AN INFANT!
    SWADDLED IN A COTTON BLANKET!

WE DO NOT TAMPER WITH THIS!

WE DO NOT TAMPER WITH GOD'S WILL!

SMOTE OUT THE SYPHILITIC EYES OF THE
HELLION!

WHAT GLOOMY, NEFARIOUS FOREST!

HAS THIS JERICHO EMERGED FROM?!

SMOTE OUT HIS EYES AND PROTECT THE
CHILDREN!

TAMI *curtsies and return to her seat.*

OTTO Well, that was certainly spirited. Thank you, Tami. Mr.
Falmouth?

TOBIN *steps up to the lectern. He is not moving so well.*

TOBIN Hi. Um. I apologize in advance if I seem a little out of
it. As you can probably see, I sort of had a, well, a rough
night and . . . well, I had blood in my urine when I woke
up this morning, and I might have some serious damage
to my ribs . . . Okay. I'll try to make this brief. To be
completely honest, I haven't prepared anything, and I'm
almost positive that my prose is better than my, um, public
speaking skills, so I hope this isn't too disappointing . . .
Uh, I didn't write *The Metal Children* for any particular
reason. I was still in my twenties, and things weren't going
so well for me. My wife and I were living in this little studio
apartment on the Lower East Side of New York with mice

and roaches, and sometimes you'd walk in and there'd be this homeless guy with a German shepherd sleeping on the kitchen floor. His name was Mr. Hudson Valley King—at least that's what he called himself—and his dog's name was Steak Knife, and sometimes they were there and sometimes they weren't, and Mr. Hudson Valley King claimed that he had an understanding with the building, like theoretically he and the building were somehow in spiritual cahoots, and then Steak Knife got run over by the M-9 crosstown bus and we never saw that guy again. It was that kind of place, and that's sort of what a lot of New York was like back in the early nineties when my wife and I moved there from Iowa City.

It was the winter—late January, I think—and our apartment was freezing and I hadn't been writing much and I was working for this company that moves office furniture and I had thrown my back out and I was pretty much just lying on the floor a lot and watching cable access and continuously ingesting this intense narcotic painkiller called hydrocodone. Well, I got addicted to the stuff and when I ran out my doctor wouldn't write me another prescription and I got pretty irritable and I was having a hard time going to the bathroom and I couldn't get an erection and I was crying all the time and sort of seriously considering hanging myself with an extension cord because I thought my wife was sleeping with this Polish guy named Witold who lived down the hall even though she wasn't and then she got pregnant and I thought it was his and I got really paranoid and hired this private detective to follow her around and Witold threatened me in the hall with a ball-peen hammer and Miranda and I started fighting a lot and she decided she didn't want the baby because I was being so mean or because she lost faith in the world or because of the Oklahoma City bombing and the Ebola virus and that huge earthquake in Japan so we went to this clinic on the Upper East Side and I was really needing pills like so bad that I was downing entire bottles of Robitussin with codeine and chasing it with large amounts of vodka and the clinic had all these fake trees in the waiting area and when Miranda came out of the room after the procedure she looked so sad and lost that I passed out and when I was in the hospital I had this dream that Miranda had turned into a statue, one of those ones where water is always running out of it; it was running out of her nose and eyes and in the dream I had to carry her up and down this flight of stairs with all of this smashed fruit everywhere like melons and pears and grapes and the heads of dead animals like goats and rabbits and other animals with snouts and the statue of my wife was unbearably heavy and the water from her nose was running everywhere and mixing with the fruit and the animal heads and I kept slipping and I almost dropped her and then I did and when she hit the bottom of the stairs she turned into a gorilla with a sword and she kept yelling things in foreign languages like *"No me moleste!"* and things in French and German too and when I woke up I couldn't stop thinking about dropping her how wet the statue got and how I lost my grip and I called the nurse and I asked them to bring me some paper and a pen and I started writing right there in my hospital bed and I didn't stop writing for six months and it became *The Metal Children*.

Well, it wound up saving my marriage. I had to do this weekend rehab program to kick the painkiller-and-vodka cocktails, and it took a long time to get back on good terms with my wife, but we stuck it out and liked each other for a long time after that, and I truly think that writing that book made us somehow closer, and then it got published and did pretty well, and the rest is history.

I wasn't trying to say anything special. I don't even know that *I* completely understand the novel. All I know is that I wrote it because I had to. At least it came out *feeling that way*, like it was an important thing for me to do. I could have just as easily built a shed or moved a pile of bricks. To be honest, I still don't how I feel about abortion. All I know is it made my wife really sad. And we had a hard time being intimate with each other for a long time after that.

The irony is that sixty-four days ago she left me. I count the days like I'm in prison or something—pretty pathetic, right? And now she's with this guy who didn't go through any of that stuff with her. And I miss her. I really miss her . . . so much . . .

Vera, I'm sorry to say that I wasn't intending to hold a mirror up. I think some very smart critics wrote some very sophisticated interpretations about what all the symbolism means in *The Metal Children* and how it relates to the

problems of today and all my skillful figurative leaps and all
that, but the truth is, I was just writing because I had to and
that's the way it came out.

EDITH DUNDEE *enters, in shock, short of breath.*

TOBIN Hello, Edith.

EDITH Terrible accident . . . There was a terrible accident . . .
They just found Stacey Kinsella . . . in the quarry . . . He
was driving your truck, Mr. Falmouth . . . He was driving
your truck.

Lights fade.

SCENE 2

An intensive care unit hospital room. There are two beds, one unoccupied. In the other bed, STACEY KINSELLA *is lying on his back, in a full-body cast, a leg in traction.* TOBIN *is seated next to him, reading* The Metal Children.

STACEY *stirs, wakes. He speaks as someone does who drifts in and out of the fog of pain medication.*

STACEY "The moon on that statue. That odd, mollusky, imperfect moon whose light silvered her soft iron edges as if God himself were suddenly deeming her flesh again. And the corn leaning away from it all. The tall, knowing corn turning blue under the night sky. Where had Meredith Elizabeth Miller of two thirty-four Raynor Road gone? Were those eyes her eyes? Had she traded in her life to a secret meadow of shadows? Had her soul turned to some mysterious ore not mined or quarried, but willed into the world by her unborn child?" It's pure poetry, Mr. Falmouth.

TOBIN Thanks, Stacey . . . How are you?

STACEY Oh, I've been better. I can't really feel my feet too well . . . Or my legs, for that matter. Everything below the waist seems to have gone away . . . Sorry about your truck.

TOBIN Don't be. It was a rental.

STACEY I don't know what happened. I think another car was trying to pass me. The road was wet. The light coming through the back windshield was blinding. Another car was coming toward me, and I swerved. That's the last thing I remember.

TOBIN The doctor said you're lucky to be alive.

Beat.

STACEY How did things go at the school board meeting?

TOBIN As well as can be expected, I guess. I don't think I did much good. You were missed.

STACEY Did they reinstate the book?

TOBIN No. At least not that I've heard. All those copies are still in the vault . . . I'm really sorry, Stacey.

STACEY Don't be sorry, Mr. Falmouth. I'm sure your presence alone meant a lot. It was good of you to come.

TOBIN Your fellow Midlothians seem pretty agitated.

STACEY You wrote a provocative novel, Mr. Falmouth. Not many people have the courage to take such a big, unflinching swing at the status quo.

TOBIN I never wanted to hurt anyone.

STACEY So you roughed us up a bit. What's a little pain? (*half joking, referring to the morphine apparatus*) That's why there's morphine.

TOBIN That's actually Dilaudid. Lucky bastard.

STACEY I'd like to think the bumps and bruises build character.

TOBIN I guess lately I feel that that's what I've lost.

STACEY Your character?

TOBIN Yes, that, but something more. My center . . . My soul.

STACEY You know, I read *The Metal Children* in one sitting. Started it on a Friday after school, finished it early Saturday morning on my living room sofa. Didn't eat, didn't drink. I don't even know that I breathed. The book read me, Mr. Falmouth . . . A person who creates such uncompromising beauty is not without a soul, I assure you . . . "You don't *have* a soul. You *are* a soul. You have a *body*."

TOBIN Who said that?

STACEY C. S. Lewis. Another great YA author.

TOBIN Wasn't he a Christian?

STACEY Yeah, but he was an atheist until the age of thirty-three. And he also happened to write arguably the best series of fantasy novels in the history of children's literature.

TOBIN No comment.

STACEY Have you read *The Chronicles of Narnia*?

TOBIN Yeah, about halfway through *The Lion, the Witch and the Wardrobe* I developed an insatiable attraction to Jadis, the White Witch. My mom took the book away from me after she caught me masturbating to an interpretive drawing of Jadis inappropriately touching Edmund aboard a snowmobile.

STACEY Whoa. That's complicated.

TOBIN Yeah, the snowmobile was also half waterbed.

STACEY That's so seventies . . . I thought Aslan was hot.

TOBIN You were attracted to a lion?

STACEY I used to keep a poster of him above my bed. My

parents were thrilled that I was reading. Little did they know . . . Hey, would you read to me?

TOBIN Um, sure. What part?

STACEY The section where Meredith tries to tell her dad she's pregnant. It's such a beautiful chapter.

TOBIN You want me to read the whole chapter?

STACEY Just the bit in her father's study. I think it's around page 150, maybe 152.

TOBIN (*turning to the page, reading from the book*) "Wade Miller's study was as clean as a church. He had recently revarnished the floor and it smelled strongly of lacquer and pipe smoke.

" 'Daddy,' Meredith said, standing at the threshold, 'can I come in?'

" 'Of course,' he replied, pushing his reading glasses off his nose.

"Meredith eased into the room as if she were easing into a warm, muddy pond, unsure of each step. Normally she would have taken the chair opposite her father, the old wooden chair from the kitchen, the one with the wobbly leg. But she elected to stand because she was seized with the feeling that if she sat, she may never get back up.

" 'What is it, sweetheart?' Wade Miller asked. His face looked oddly huge to Meredith. Huge and kind and terrible. His black whiskers seemingly had doubled since she'd gotten home from school. She could hardly bear the thought of his disappointment.

" 'I'm pregnant,' she heard herself say.

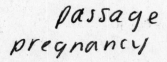
passage
pregnancy

"Her own voice sounded tinny and faraway, as if it were being broadcast from the small transistor fishing radio on the shelf behind her father, a shelf containing Wade's prized top water lures and a framed picture of him and his daughter proudly holding an enormous bass they'd caught the summer before on Cork Lake. *My legs were so thin and pale*, Meredith thought. *Not even a year ago, I still looked like a child.*

"When Wade Miller stood, he was as big as a giant. He was barely six feet tall, but when he reached his full height, to Meredith he appeared suddenly monstrous, too large for his study, as if he might burst through the ceiling.

" 'Daddy?' she said.

"When Wade Miller opened his mouth, nothing came out. The only sound was the small metal Swiss Army clock clipping time at the edge of his desk. Each tick-tock was like a needle jabbing at Meredith's heart. She wasn't sure what her father was going to do or say. His brown eyes seemed enormous and deep and loving.

"*Love me*, she thought. *Please just love me.*"

EDITH DUNDEE *enters, holding a bouquet of flowers.* TOBIN *sees her, stops reading.*

EDITH Mr. Falmouth.

TOBIN Hi, Edith.

EDITH I didn't mean to interrupt.

TOBIN (*closing the book*) You're not interrupting.

EDITH How is he?

TOBIN He's hanging in there. (*realizes* STACEY *has fallen asleep*)

EDITH Everyone at the high school's just worried sick. (*she sets the flowers down*) What have they told you?

TOBIN He broke a femur, both tibias, an ulna, his clavicle, dislocated his sternum, and cracked seven ribs.

EDITH What about his faculties? Are his faculties okay? It would be such a shame if he couldn't teach again. His students just think the world of him.

A NURSE *enters, uses a penlight to check* STACEY'*s pupils.*

EDITH Are his faculties okay?

NURSE Are you the next of kin?

EDITH No. I'm just a friend.

NURSE I'm afraid the doctor is the only one who can answer that question.

EDITH Oh. Well, is he around?

NURSE He should be by shortly.

The NURSE *exits, writing on the clipboard.*

EDITH Did you hear about Tami Lake?

TOBIN What happened to Tami Lake?

EDITH She disappeared last night. And this morning there was a statue of her erected in front of the library . . . There was a brass plate on the front. Guess what it says?

TOBIN "Gone for now"?

EDITH Sort of makes you wonder.

TOBIN Wonder what exactly?

EDITH Well, Mr. Falmouth, if one follows the rules of your book . . .

TOBIN Maybe she's at a friend's house.

EDITH I don't think Tami has many friends.

TOBIN Then someone's obviously playing a joke.

EDITH Pretty cruel joke.

TOBIN Hopefully she'll turn up.

Pause.

EDITH Mr. Falmouth, I should tell you that my niece has gone missing too. Vera never came home last night.

TOBIN I'm sorry to hear that, Edith.

EDITH Officer Tidwell suggested that I file a missing person's report, but it all just seems so unlikely. You haven't seen her, have you?

TOBIN I'm afraid I haven't.

EDITH I just hope another one of those statues doesn't turn up.

TOBIN Your niece is a resourceful girl, Edith.

EDITH That's true. Vera certainly is resourceful.

TOBIN I'm sure she's okay.

EDITH I really hope so, Mr. Falmouth. I really, really do hope so.

She watches STACEY in the hospital bed.

EDITH Get well, Mr. Kinsella. (*to* TOBIN) Well, I suppose I should go. (*handing him a card*) If there's any news, will you call the motel?

TOBIN *nods.*

EDITH *exits. He places her card in his pocket, stands over* STACEY *in the hospital bed, watching him for a moment, then reaches down and gently wipes his brow with the back of his hand as lights fade.*

SCENE 3

Middle of the night. The town square. The steps of the library.
A statue of a young woman on a two-foot base. There is a brass
plate that reads GONE FOR NOW. *Several small candles have been*
arranged around it, as well as scores of flowers. TOBIN *is seated on*
some steps.

ROBERTA CUPP *emerges from the shadows.*

ROBERTA About an hour ago they found her hanging in
the basement of the Good Church of Christ. She was
an A student. First-chair flautist. She loved her church.
Volunteered at the senior center twice a week. She had
hopes of becoming a special ed teacher. Sixteen years old.

TOBIN I don't know what to say. I'm stunned.

ROBERTA I think we all are . . . She was six weeks pregnant,
Mr. Falmouth.

TOBIN The baby?

ROBERTA It's in a petri dish over at the hospital if you want to
go take a look.

TOBIN Do they know who the father was?

ROBERTA No . . . At this point only a handful of people know
about the hanging. And if you're wondering where the
statue came from, your guess is as good as anybody's.

OTTO HURLEY *enters with a rosary.*

OTTO Hi, Roberta.

ROBERTA Hello, Otto.

OTTO (*to* TOBIN) Mr. Falmouth.

TOBIN Hey.

OTTO (*hanging the rosary on the hand of the statue*) You know,
I finally got a chance to read your book. You're a heck of a
writer.

TOBIN Thanks.

OTTO The characters. The way you tell a story. Gripping stuff.

TOBIN I'm surprised you feel that way.

OTTO (*still with the statue*) Oh, me too, Mr. Falmouth, me too.
But if this is what happens to people who read your work,
you might want to seriously consider another vocation. (*to*
ROBERTA) Take care, Roberta.

ROBERTA You too, Otto.

OTTO *exits.* ROBERTA *crosses to the steps, sits.*

ROBERTA Rough night, huh?

TOBIN You could say that.

ROBERTA At least you can hear the crickets. They're early this
year. The sound of crickets always seems to calm me.

TOBIN In New York we have the sound of garbage trucks.

ROBERTA I can't even imagine it.

TOBIN You get used to it just like anything else.

ROBERTA I s'pose you would.

Beat.

TOBIN Can I ask you a question, Roberta?

ROBERTA I don't see why not.

TOBIN You ever been married?

ROBERTA I was, yes. He passed away seven years ago.

TOBIN What was his name?

ROBERTA His name was James. James Garrison Cupp. He
was a foreman at the power plant, and he had a very long
bout with throat cancer. But in the end God took him
peacefully.

TOBIN I'm sorry to hear that.

ROBERTA It's hard losing the ones we love. But we move on.
It's all part of God's plan.

Beat.

ROBERTA That story you told at the assembly about your wife
was sad. Losing a child is tragic.

TOBIN We didn't lose it; we aborted it.

ROBERTA Well, that's even more heartbreaking.

TOBIN Yeah, the whole situation was pretty painful.

ROBERTA James and I never had kids.

TOBIN Didn't want 'em?

ROBERTA No, we were incapable. We thought about adopting,
but then he got sick.

TOBIN Life sucks and then you drink. That's my motto.

Beat.

ROBERTA Mr. Falmouth, have you ever considered the possibility of Jesus Christ in your life?

TOBIN You know, Roberta, I have, yes. But when it comes right down to it, I can never seem to get past the fact that he has a such a striking resemblance to Richard Chamberlain in *The Thorn Birds*.

ROBERTA And here I thought we were having a real conversation.

TOBIN We weren't having a conversation?

ROBERTA I was simply asking a question. Jesus Christ happens to be a big part of my life. You resort to mockery.

TOBIN Don't suddenly start acting like you're my friend, Roberta.

ROBERTA Why not?

TOBIN Because a few hours ago I was the visiting werewolf from New York City and you were damning my novel to hell. And now I'm suddenly a potential Christian?

ROBERTA The truth is that I'm often drawn to those who need it most.

TOBIN Oh, spare me the horseshit, Roberta! I'm not that fucking desperate!

ROBERTA Coulda fooled me.

TOBIN Why don't you go wiggle off in your shapeless denim jumper and work on beefing up your conversion quota somewhere else.

ROBERTA Mr. Falmouth, be warned. Do indeed be warned. When the news breaks tomorrow morning, I imagine there will be some angry Midlothians looking for a certain visiting author. And things could get quite ugly, they certainly could, yes. If I were you, I would consider finding yourself some reliable form of transportation and getting out of here as fast as possible.

TOBIN Is that a threat or a prophecy?

ROBERTA How can you be so smug? After what's happened to that poor girl? You with your pathetic, self-indulgent self-pity slung around your neck like a bag of rotting feces. You should be ashamed of yourself!

TOBIN Trust me, I'm not.

ROBERTA Do you have any idea what her parents must be going through? Who do you people think you are? You *artists*. So high and mighty. Amoral. Stuck-up, godless hobgoblins floating above it all in your mischievous hot-air balloons. Poking fun. Turning your noses up at everything. Poking fun at good, decent people. Well, I'll tell you something, Mr. Falmouth, with your frumpy old-man clothes and noisome disposition, I'll tell you something right here and now. God does not appreciate what you are doing, no, He does not. In fact, I would go so far as to say He abhors it. Flaunting your condescension at the rest of the world like some baboon's swollen anus! Lucifer walks among us and wheedles about on hooved feet. Though we do not see him, he is in our lives. He is in our livestock and our water supply, and he hides behind our oldest trees. And now it is clear to me that he is in our books too.

TOBIN Why don't you go make a fucking pamphlet or something?

ROBERTA Oh, I will, Mr. Falmouth. You better believe I will. And I will *keep* making them until our world is free of the filth—the paste, the film, the wicked venereal sludge—that people like you put on this planet!

TOBIN Roberta, look, I could sit here and you could stand there and we could probably do this all night. But I'm tired. I've had two of the worst days of my life. My rental car got totaled. Stacey Kinsella is hanging on by a thread at the hospital. I have blood in my urine, a deviated septum, I'm walking around with bruised and possibly broken ribs, and some poor girl killed herself. I just want to sit here, okay? Is that too much to ask? I just want to sit here and like *breathe* for a moment. Because Jesus *doesn't* love me, I'm afraid. No, the anorectic, vaguely bearded one does not love yours truly. Nor does his enigmatic invisible father. If the fucker actually exists, he probably doesn't even *like* me. So what do I have to lose, right? What do I have to lose that I already haven't?

The BOY IN THE PORKY PIG MASK *enters, runs up to* TOBIN, *violently stabs him in the stomach with a large hunting knife as* ROBERTA CUPP *looks on.*

Blackout.

SCENE 4

STACEY KINSELLA's *ICU room.* STACEY *is still motionless in his bed, still in traction. In the other bed,* TOBIN *lies on his back, wearing a hospital gown. An IV has been fed into his arm. He is on narcotic medication, and his stomach is bandaged.* VERA DUNDEE, *no longer painted gold, is seated beside him. She is holding a small pad of paper and a pen. On the other side of him, sitting on the floor, is a freshman boy.* TOBIN *wakes. He is weak and speaks as might one who floats in and out of clouds of morphine.*

TOBIN Vera.

VERA I couldn't leave without saying goodbye. We're all just so happy you're alive . . . Can I get you anything?

TOBIN Maybe some water.

She pours him some water, helps him drink with a straw, sits.

VERA Apparently the knife was less than a centimeter from severing your aorta.

TOBIN Must be my bottomless well of recent good luck . . . You know your aunt's been looking for you. She's worried sick. I told her I'd call the motel if I saw you.

VERA Please don't.

TOBIN She's worried sick, Vera.

VERA She'll be fine.

Beat.

TOBIN (*to* VERA) How long you been here?

BOY X About an hour.

TOBIN (*referring to the* BOY) Who's he?

VERA He's Boy X. Our donor. He wanted to meet you.

BOY X Hi, Mr. Falmouth.

TOBIN Hi, Boy X.

BOY X *hurls himself to the floor at* TOBIN*'s bedside, genuflects, bows his head, grasps* TOBIN*'s hand, groans with passion and grief.*

TOBIN So I guess I keep pissing off Porky Pig. (*to* BOY X)
    Whatever you do, don't piss off Porky Pig.

BOY X I won't, Mr. Falmouth.

BOY X *sits back.*

TOBIN (*to* VERA) Last time I saw you, you were painted gold.
    How was the vigil?

VERA It was good. We pissed some parents off. Cooper's dad
    grounded her in front of everyone, and she told him to go
    take his Viagra and watch *Gossip Girl*, so that part was fun.
    Eventually the cops made us leave, but we made our point.

TOBIN When are you planning on leaving for Idaho?

VERA Tonight. The first van left a few hours ago. Sick letters were forged and delivered to the principal's office before first period. Most parents won't even know we're gone till dinnertime.

TOBIN (*to* BOY x) What about you? Are you going too?

BOY x The movement needs me.

TOBIN Lucky you.

Beat.

VERA You know, you talk in your sleep.

TOBIN I do?

VERA Yes. And with surprising clarity.

TOBIN What was I saying?

BOY x You were having a conversation with your wife.

TOBIN Miranda.

VERA She's pretty, isn't she?

TOBIN Yeah, she's pretty.

VERA You say her name like she is.

TOBIN Was our conversation terrifically one-sided and borderline misogynistic?

VERA No.

TOBIN Was she employing more effective active verbs?

VERA It wasn't like that.

TOBIN What was it like?

VERA It was actually really sad and sweet. You performed both parts. With two distinct voices. You asked her if she left you because you got ugly, and she said that that was ridiculous and childishly reductive and that she *had* to leave because you were both so unhappy for so long.

TOBIN And then what?

VERA And then you told her it was probably best because she was starting to write you under the table, but you said that part sort of ironically, and then she told you as much.

TOBIN She told me I was being ironic?

VERA She said you were being bionically ironic . . . And then she said your name very gently and told you that she was going to marry someone named Steve—

BOY X And that she wanted a divorce.

VERA And that part was hard for her to say . . . And then you got sad and cried in your sleep. It sounded like a toy train whistling in a basement.

A young nurse enters.

NURSE How you feeling?

TOBIN Okay.

NURSE If you need more for the pain, just press the button.

The nurse crosses to STACEY KINSELLA.

TOBIN How's he doing?

NURSE Better. He's a fighter, this one.

She exits.

TOBIN Then what?

VERA Then you asked her if she really loved him.

TOBIN Steve.

VERA Yes, Steve.

TOBIN And she said . . .

BOY X She said that she did.

VERA And then you asked her if he made her laugh, and she said yes.

BOY X And then you asked her if he had better toenails.

VERA And she said yes again and laughed while she said it. And then you asked her if he had good cholesterol and plenty of fiber in his diet, and she said yes to both and that his health was excellent.

TOBIN That's five yeses in a row.

VERA It's actually six if you count cholesterol and fiber as separate dietary constructs.

TOBIN You should see the guy. It's like I'm up against Luke Skywalker.

VERA Then you asked her if he makes her cry when she comes like you could, but she didn't answer that . . . and after a long pause she said she didn't want the divorce to be a big mess.

BOY X And then you told her you missed her and cried some more.

TOBIN Was I really doing both voices?

VERA/BOY X Yes.

TOBIN She has a really nice Midwestern accent . . . Anything else?

VERA You asked her if the two of you would have made it if you hadn't lost the baby.

TOBIN And what did she say?

VERA I don't know because that's when you woke up . . . I wrote most of it down if you'd like to have a copy of it.

TOBIN You keep it.

VERA Mr. Falmouth, are you going to continue to write? I only ask because whether you like it or not, you do it with tremendous power, and it would be a disservice to us all if you decided to stop.

TOBIN thinks for a moment.

TOBIN I don't know, Vera. I honestly don't know.

Lights fade.

SCENE 5

TOBIN's *apartment, late February, the following winter. His place is in much better shape, cleaner, picked up.* BRUNO *is sitting on* TOBIN's *couch, reading the last few pages of a large manuscript;* TOBIN *paces behind him. A quiet intensity has been thickening for some time.* BRUNO *turns over the last page, sits there.* TOBIN *is frozen in anticipation. After a long pause:*

BRUNO It's brilliant.

TOBIN Really?

BRUNO I'm speechless . . . The fucking thing gallops, Tobin.

TOBIN You really think it's good?

BRUNO I forgot that I was on your sofa. Talk about a rabbit hole. That was time travel.

TOBIN And those weird drawings are okay?

BRUNO The drawings are amazing! The man crying at the feet of the robot. The McDonald's special sauce oozing out of the civic leader's open wound. It's like *Breakfast of Champions* meets Edward Gorey or something.

TOBIN And the guy walking backwards through the Red Lobster with the crucifix isn't too obvious?

BRUNO Fuck obvious. Who cares about obvious? It's unbridled, and it's your best work. Fucking depressing as hell, in its indictment of middle-American conformist

consumerism and the fear of otherness, but your best work.
And the whole town stoning that kid to death with Duracell
batteries . . .

TOBIN You like that.

BRUNO I love it.

TOBIN Will it work as a YA?

BRUNO Oh, it's an adult book. No doubt about it. I'm calling
Nan at Scribner as soon as I get back to the office—she'll
fucking love this. And then I'll call David at Viking just to
spice things up a bit. Hatch ourselves a bidding war . . . I'm
really proud of you.

TOBIN Thanks, Bruno.

Beat.

BRUNO So not to tamper with a celebratory mood, but are you
going to the wedding?

TOBIN No.

BRUNO But she invited you, right?

TOBIN She did. I burned the invitation. First I tore it into
sixteenths, then I pissed on it, then I burned it. I never
knew urine was flammable.

BRUNO It's understandable.

TOBIN Are you going?

BRUNO Not if you're not.

TOBIN I hope he leaves her for some M.F.A. Brown grad with
a thousand-page manuscript and perfect tits.

BRUNO We move on. (*referring to the manuscript*) New

horizons, right? We sell this bad boy and get you a summer home somewhere. I see you on the Cape in one of those old houses with a porch swing. Big bay window. Waterfront view. The front lawn charmingly overrun with dandelions.

TOBIN Yeah, me, myself, and I, all alone with all my dandelions.

BRUNO Who gets married in February, anyway? That's so, I don't know, like Dr. Zhivago or something. And at the Puck Building, no less. I can just see it: the publishing elite and their boring, bloodless dates, drinking hot buttered rum and fucking freezing to death in the grand ballroom.

TOBIN Maybe they're meant to be together.

BRUNO Maybe they are, Tobin.

A sad silence.

BRUNO (*patting the manuscript*) Hey, congratulations, huh? In a little less than a year, you live through a brutal stabbing, *The Metal Children* is famously banned, makes the bestseller list, you get a very nice feature in the *Times*, write yet another brilliant book—decidedly for adults, mind you— and manage to clean up your apartment. Things eventually change for the better, right?

TOBIN I guess they do.

BRUNO I'll let you know how my conversation with Nan goes. My prediction is that seventy-two hours from now we'll be sitting in the Oak Room of the Algonquin Hotel, drinking Dom Pérignon out of the bottle.

BRUNO *crosses to exit with the manuscript, opens the front door.*

VERA DUNDEE, *dressed in winter clothes, carrying a backpack, and holding a bundled infant in her arms, is standing in the entrance. She seems lost, exhausted. Her hair, under a scarf, is darker, back to its natural color.*

BRUNO Hi.

VERA Hi.

BRUNO Speaking of Dr. Zhivago.

TOBIN Vera.

VERA Hello, Mr. Falmouth.

TOBIN Vera, this is Bruno, my agent.

VERA Nice to meet you.

BRUNO Likewise.

TOBIN Vera was the young Midlothian woman who started the petition to save *The Metal Children.*

BRUNO Tobin speaks very highly of you. Unfortunately the book has been permanently struck from the curriculum, but you should still be proud of yourself. It was brave of you to lead the charge.

VERA That book has changed a lot of lives.

BRUNO Let's hope the new one does too. (*referring to the baby*) Who's that?

VERA Celia.

BRUNO Hi, Celia. How old is she?

VERA Ten weeks. (*to* TOBIN) Can I come in?

TOBIN Of course.

She enters. There is an awkward silence.

VERA I'd love to have some time alone with Mr. Falmouth, if
that's okay.
BRUNO Tobin?
TOBIN It's fine.
BRUNO You sure?

TOBIN *nods.*

BRUNO I'll call you later.

BRUNO *exits with the manuscript.*

TOBIN What a surprise.
VERA Yeah.
TOBIN How did you get in the building?
VERA Front door was open. Would you mind if I sat down?
TOBIN Not at all. Here, sit.

He clears something off the sofa. She sits with the baby.

TOBIN Something to drink?
VERA I'd love a glass of water.
TOBIN Sure.

He exits, returns with a glass of water, hands it to her.

VERA Thanks.

She drinks, sets the glass down.

VERA So this is where you live. I imagined it messier.

TOBIN It's taken me about six months to get the place into shape. I hired this entire administrative team to come organize things. It was like watching an archaeology dig. Three long days of sifting through piles that should never be named.

VERA You look good.

TOBIN Yeah, I joined a gym. Lost some weight. I eat better. Stopped drinking.

VERA Good for you.

TOBIN I just finished a novel too. Last night actually. The sun was coming up while I was typing the last paragraph. It was sort of a cliché.

VERA Congratulations. Is it for young adults?

TOBIN No. So I won't have to deal with any of those lovely curriculums this time.

Awkward pause.

TOBIN So how have you been?

VERA I've been well. I don't sleep much.

TOBIN I was gonna say, you look a little tired. She keeping you up at night?

VERA At the community my sisters help me out, but you never really rest. There's just so much to do.

TOBIN The community. That's still going strong?

VERA I brought pictures.

She goes into the backpack, removes snapshots.

VERA That's the farmhouse there. And the barn where we keep the hens and make the T-shirts. There's two acres of land that we're learning how to farm on. That's our first stand of corn, there, see? That's Genie Brazil on a tractor that we found abandoned on a nearby dirt road. Dinner is at seven-thirty every night. That's where we eat. We made that table out of an old silo door. And that's a group shot of all the sisters. And those are the children.

TOBIN Is the boy still with you?

VERA Yes, although I think he's getting a little tired of being around us all the time. He helps a lot with the children.

Awkward pause.

VERA New York is so big. So noisy.

TOBIN It must be quite a shock compared to Idaho.

VERA So many people on the street.

Awkward pause.

VERA Can I ask you a question, Mr. Falmouth?

TOBIN Sure.

VERA Do you ever think about me?

TOBIN I do, yeah. I mean I have.

VERA Really?

TOBIN Yes, really.

VERA Because I think about you.

TOBIN You do?

VERA Yes.

TOBIN In what way?

VERA I wonder if you're okay. What your day is like. If you're writing. If I take up any space in your head . . . Do I, Mr. Falmouth?

TOBIN Do you what.

VERA Take up space in your head?

TOBIN *hesitates.*

VERA Not even in a vague way?

TOBIN Vera, we only knew each other for a few days.

VERA But what happened between us was . . .

TOBIN It was what.

VERA . . . important.

TOBIN It was almost a year ago. This is the first time I've heard as much as a peep from you.

VERA Have you even looked at our website?

TOBIN Of course I have.

VERA You keep up with our mission?

TOBIN Yes.

VERA What happened between us was epic . . .

She fades off somehow.

TOBIN You sure you're okay, Vera?

VERA Can I use your bathroom?

TOBIN It's down the hall, to your right.

VERA Would you mind holding her for a second?

TOBIN Not at all.

She hands him the baby, exits to the bathroom with her backpack. He stares at the baby.

TOBIN Hello . . . Hello, little Celia . . . Look at you . . . Look at you . . .

VERA *reenters, watches him with the baby.*

VERA What's that saying on your bathroom mirror? "Be Here Now."

TOBIN It's just something to remind me to stay in the moment, keep things simple. I go to meetings. Affirmations are good. I see that on my mirror and I say, "Tobin, be here now." It sounds silly, I'm sure, but it really does help.

VERA She has your eyes.

TOBIN She's beautiful.

VERA She was born December seventh. I had her naturally, in a twenty-four-inch birthing pool of boiled well water. It was a brief labor, only four hours. My doula drove over a hundred miles to be with me. She lives with us now and has grown to be passionate about the movement. Our daughter slid out of me effortlessly and swam in place like an otter. When we pulled her out of the water, she didn't cry; she chirped. Celia means "heaven," whose origin is from the Latin *caelum*. We call her our little bird from heaven. Her middle name is Meredith.

TOBIN You should have told me about this, Vera.

VERA I'm not here to make you take responsibility for her. At least not in any conventional way.

TOBIN Then why are you here?

VERA The community has fallen on hard times, Mr. Falmouth. We started out very strong. We had three very successful births. Two boys and a girl. Then we lost a child. A little girl who was born without a mouth. She lived for about three hours, and then her heart stopped. Then twin boys were born. Carl and Calvin. Celia was the sixth. Of the thirty-six girls who made the trip, only fourteen have stayed on, and while the selling of Meredith Miller merchandise through our website PayPal system helps us maintain good standing on our mortgage, we don't have enough for proper food and care for the children. We have to replace the clay tile lining of our well because it is contaminated. One of the twins, Calvin, had a terrible ear infection. We drove him to a clinic in Boise, but it took too long because the transmission in our 1987 Buick LeSabre is faulty. And little Calvin's deaf now. So there will be signing lessons to deal with. And while we were able to farm our own food in the summer and early fall, we've run out, and we're currently subsisting on rice and eggs.

TOBIN So you're here asking for money.

VERA Anything you could do would be a huge help.

He says nothing.

VERA *The Metal Children* is obviously doing very well since that article ran in the *Times*. It's been on the bestseller list for thirty-two consecutive weeks, and I am also aware of a film deal that was struck for a sizable sum.

TOBIN What if I want to be in her life?

VERA In what capacity?

TOBIN In the capacity that she's my daughter.

VERA Well, there's obviously a lot to discuss.

TOBIN Do I need to call my lawyer?

VERA Of course not.

TOBIN *continues holding the baby.*

VERA Maybe you could come out to McCall and spend some time with us? We've been pretty strict about not letting outsiders visit, but you're obviously an exception to the rule.

Awkward pause.

VERA We have four births scheduled for next week, Mr. Falmouth, and your cooperation couldn't be timelier.

TOBIN *hands* VERA *the baby, exits.* VERA *crosses to the window with* CELIA, *peers down at the street, sings a quiet song to her.* TOBIN *reenters with a checkbook. He writes a check as the dialogue continues.*

VERA (*from the window*) Are those kids down there homeless?

TOBIN If by "homeless" you mean did they run away from Connecticut, buy some carefully distressed army fatigues, stop showering, and start shooting heroin so they can collect a few anecdotes to write about in their journals, then yes, they're homeless. Most of them will be on the train back to Greenwich by the end of the month.

TOBIN *hands* VERA *the check, drops the checkbook on the coffee table. She looks at it.*

VERA This is very generous of you, Mr. Falmouth. Thank you.

TOBIN Where are you staying tonight?

VERA At a women's shelter up on 168th Street.

TOBIN You're more than welcome to stay here. The couch pulls out.

VERA I was hoping to hand out pamphlets. Make some connections.

TOBIN The mission.

VERA The mission is my life . . . I should probably actually go soon.

TOBIN Can I have another minute with her?

VERA Would you like me to leave?

TOBIN No, you can stay. I just want to hold her again.

VERA *gives him the baby, sits.*

TOBIN How many times a day do you have to change her diaper?

VERA Six to eight. We use cloth diapers. It saves money.

TOBIN Does she ever get loud?

VERA At about four-thirty in the morning. She can wail with the best of 'em.

TOBIN What's her favorite thing?

VERA Well, right now she doesn't have many options. My breast milk would have to rank up there at the top of the list. She also seems to respond to the colors blue and green. And she likes the sound that the hens make when we basket their eggs.

TOBIN The other girls are nice to her?

VERA They love her, Mr. Falmouth. She's loved.

TOBIN Is she really my daughter?

VERA Yes.

TOBIN You swear to God?

VERA I don't believe in God, Mr. Falmouth, but I'll swear on my life, how's that?

VERA *watches* TOBIN *with* CELIA.

VERA I can't tell you how many times I've imagined this
     moment . . . She likes you.
TOBIN I love her.

VERA *lets him have another moment with* CELIA, *then approaches
him, takes her back.* TOBIN *writes on the back of a scrap of paper.*

TOBIN My phone number and e-mail address . . . When would
     be a good time for me to come out to Idaho?
VERA In a few months. The new children will be a lot to deal
     with until then.
TOBIN So what, May, June?
VERA Sure.
TOBIN How are you getting up to the shelter?
VERA We were going to take the bus.
TOBIN (*producing his wallet, handing her some cash*) Here, take
     a cab.

VERA *accepts the money.*

VERA Thank you.

Awkward pause.

TOBIN Okay, then. I don't know what else to say.
VERA You say it all with your work, Mr. Falmouth.

She touches his cheek in the same manner he did near the end of Act I. She then crosses to the front door, exits with CELIA.

TOBIN *sits for a moment and then starts to quietly cry as lights fade.*